THE

Cutter's Practical Guide

TO

CUTTING AND MAKING

BODY COATS

Bibliografische Information der Deutschen Nationalbibliothek:
Die Deutsche Nationalbibliothek verzeichnet diese Publikation
in der Deutschen Nationalbibliografie; detaillierte bibliografische
Daten sind im Internet über www.dnb.de abrufbar.

Reprint of the original from 1890
© 2025
Republished by Sven Jungclaus
https://www.becomeatailor.com

Verlag:
BoD · Books on Demand GmbH, In de Tarpen 42, 22848 Norderstedt,
bod@bod.de
Druck:
Libri Plureos GmbH, Friedensallee 273, 22763 Hamburg
ISBN: 978-3-7583-5047-4

PRACTICAL GUIDE

TO CUTTING

Every kind of Garment made by Tailors

With detailed instructions as to their production.

PART II.

Body Coats of every description, embracing Morning, Frock and Dress Coats, Livery, Clerical, Naval, Military, Police, and many other Special Garments.

BY W. D. F. VINCENT.

Author of " The Cutter's Album." " Guide to the use of Model Patterns," &c.

PRINTED AND PUBLISHED BY THE JOHN WILLIAMSON COMPANY LIMITED, AT *THE TAILOR AND CUTTER* OFFICE, 93 & 94 DRURY LANE, LONDON, W.C.

"W.D.F. Vincent was born in Junie 1860 and began his career as an apprentice with Frederick Cooper in Yeovil. After completing his training, he briefly established his own businesses in Oxford and later in Maidenhead as a clothier and tailor, though neither venture was financially successful.

While in Maidenhead, Vincent won an essay competition on tailoring, which was open to all members of the National Federation of Foremen Tailors, titled "The Great National Work on Trouser Cutting, or Defects in Trousers." He submitted his entry under the pseudonym "Oxonian" and won the first prize. This success led him to secure a position with The Tailor and Cutter magazine. In the early years, Vincent contributed numerous articles on tailoring methods and techniques to the magazine. However, due to the terms of his employment, these articles were published without attribution to him.

By the 1890s, Vincent became a leading tailoring authority. His books, such as The Cutter's Practical Guide to the Cutting & Making of All Kinds of Trousers, became standard reference work. By 1917, Vincent referred to himself as a journalist. He died in June 1926.

The Tailor and Cutter magazine and academy were operated by John Williamson & Co Ltd. In the 1950s and 1960s, many tailors displayed their Tailor & Cutter Academy Diplomas, signed by W.D.F. Vincent, as the Chairman of Examiners, as a centerpiece in their shop windows. One such example can still be seen on display at the Museum of Welsh Life at St. Fagans in South Wales."

(cf. https://vincents.org.uk/family-history/w-d-f-vincent-tailor; 15.12.2024)

This edition is a reprint of the legendary *Cutter's Practical Guide* series; the first book was published in 1890. Although W. D. F. Vincent wrote many books on tailoring, these are the most popular. The entire text has been meticulously read, and the images have been carefully cleaned and edited to ensure the highest quality.

Content

PREVIOUSLY PRINTED BY THE JOHN WILLIAMSON COMPANY LIMITED,
93 & 94 DRURY LANE, LONDON, W.C.

https://www.becomeatailor.com

PUBLISHER'S PREFACE

"The Cutters' Practical Guide" being the present acknowledged Standard System of Cutting at the Tailor and Cutter Office and the System taught to the Students at our Academy, it has, in a variety of forms and adaptations, been laid before the members of the tailoring trade. The cordial reception it has met has induced us to develop both the System and its applications, and prepare these for publication in more permanent form. Part One has already appeared, in which the System is adapted more particularly to Youths' and Juvenile Garments. A promise was then made that Part Two, embracing every Style and Class of Gents' Body Coats, would ultimately be published. Considerable delay has taken place in its preparation, and oft-repeated have been the enquiries as to when it should appear. But several other works have been published by us since Part One of this work appeared, one of these being "The Practical Guide adapted to all the Current Styles of Ladies' Tailor-made Garments".

The present work will be valued, not only for its application to ordinary coats, but by many more because it embraces many garments which in most trades are regarded special and unusual. Among these we may reckon Military, Naval, and Livery garments, with other classes of official and non-official dress, which the head of every respectable firm is liable to be called upon to make.

The work throughout will be found thoroughly practical in its mode of representing and dealing with the various styles and classes of garments. Everything superfluous is studiously avoided. The work is prepared for practical Cutters and for everyday use, which will be greatly facilitated by the large clear type and equally clear engraving of the Plates. We feel confidence in placing it in the hands of our many patrons.

THE JOHN WILLIAMSON COMPANY, LIMITED.

THE
Cutter's Practical Guide
TO
CUTTING AND MAKING
EVERY KIND OF GARMENT
BODY COATS

It is nearly four years since the first article appeared in the pages of the *Tailor and Cutter* under the above title, and from a very large number of readers of that journal we have had many expressions of opinion as to their value, and asking such questions as "Can I have them all in one book?" In response to these requests we have prepared the present volume. It is based on the articles that have appeared in the pages of the *Tailor and Cutter*, with such additions as the author thinks would increase its practical value, whilst many subjects which have not yet been treated of in the serial articles, have been added so as to make the work complete.

This is a practical work for practical men and is the outcome of successful experience. The author endeavours to lay out all those little details of cutting and making before his fellow craftsmen which have really more to do with success than a vast theoretical knowledge of scientific cutting. Science has done much for the cutter, but we do not desire to study science for the sake of science. What is wanted, is science that shall help us in our every day practice, help us to fit our customers, and so help us towards success.

The subject matter of this work, is body coats in their many varieties, from a Coster's Coat to a Peer's Frock, embracing Military, Naval, Livery, Clerical and Police Garments, and as the necessary explanation of these will produce a good size volume, we will not take up space by a long introduction, but at once proceed to the work before us.

It is of the utmost importance that every cutter should be fully aware of the component parts of a coat, in order that he may be able to so vary the cut as to suit the various peculiarities of the customer he is called upon to clothe, and also to produce certain effects to meet their whims and fancies. By component parts we do not mean back, forepart, sleeve, collar, &c., but rather those quantities or sections which go to make up the various parts, and which must all be arranged in accordance with the requirements of the customer. Perhaps our readers will better understand the meaning we wish to convey, if we style them

The Principles of Coat Cutting.

It matters not what plan we adopt, whether it be breast measure, shoulder measure, direct measure, or block patterns, so long as these principles are understood, and the various quantities in each section properly regulated. We therefore begin this work by dealing with these component parts, sections, or principles, which we lay down as follows: 1st. Height of neck. 2nd. Position and size of scye. 3rd. Balance. 4th. Waist suppression. 5th. Spring over the hips. 6th. Allowance for making, ease, &c. 7th. The location of the neck point. There are several important principles involved in the sleeves, collars, &c., but the above will be quite sufficient in considering the body part. We will now proceed to deal with each of these sections, in order, as far as possible to lay a good foundation for succeeding articles.

The Height of Neck.

Many and ingenious have been the devices and arrangements for obtaining the height of neck or shoulder slope, all of which have more or less failed, with the exception of direct measures, inasmuch as this section of the body has been found to vary independently of any other; and it will at once be obvious that all those who obtain the amount of shoulder slope by a division of the breast, total height, or natural waist length, are all more or less in error, although it is only just to admit that the latter method is in the right direction, and calculated to produce results nearer the mark than any other divisional method; and had we no opportunity of obtaining the few additional measures we desire, we should not have any hesitation in fixing the height of neck by one-sixth of the natural waist, as it will be found in a very large number of cases to come very near the mark, producing squarer shoulders for a short and stout figure, and the reverse for the tall and thin. But as we said before,

this method is not to be absolutely relied upon, as in practice, we find tall figures with square shoulders, and short ones with sloping ones, and so on. Others again have taken the height of neck by measuring upwards from the level of shoulders, a plan which is certainly in advance of the last method, as it deals with this section independently of any other. Still this has been found lacking in meeting the requirements of a class of figures which are abnormally developed in the front shoulder. Hence, after examining all the various plans put before the trade, we have finally selected the over-shoulder measure as the one best calculated to meet the case, when taken in conjunction with the depth of scye on back, and the front shoulder. It is by no means a new method, being published in a work nearly seventy years ago, and as we believe it is of real practical value, we have embodied it in the system we shall lay down. Some have argued against this method, that in taking it over the coat, mistakes may often arise through the shoulders being built up with wadding and padding; but this is a difficulty to be overcome with every method, even those which mainly rely upon the aid of judgment in the use of a breast measure system. It may be truly said, that most people come to be measured in the garment they like best, and all that is necessary to meet the case is to treat the coat in the same way as the one they are wearing has been treated. But we shall point out as we proceed, that the fitting of the body is not everthing, the pleasing the customer's eye and producing a becoming garment being of even greater importance. It is easy, of course, to overcome even this padding difficulty by politely asking the customer to allow you to take his measures under the coat, a plan which we think must be followed by many firms. During our experience we have had many gentlemen proceed at once to take off their coats, and on one occasion a lady enquired if we required to measure under the bodice. Still, the number of garments with built-up shoulders form a very small minority; and whilst using every care to spot them when measuring, yet we may safely leave them to the try-on. The next section in order is

The Position and Size of Scye.

This, as everyone knows, is a very important section, for if it is not located properly, or not of the correct size, much discomfort may be felt by the wearer, and the garment certain to be returned for alteration. The methods mostly in vogue for this, are to fix its depth either by taking one-third of the scye, and adding it to one-sixth of the natural waist for the shoulder slope, or one-fourth of a scale found by taking 36 as the normal, and increasing ¼ inch for every inch below, and decreasing ¼ inch for every inch above. The depth of scye for a 24 breast would thus be 6¾, and that for a 48 11¼ both plans producing fairly satisfactory results for the ordinary-going figure, but failing to produce those variations in the balance necessary in dealing with abnormal figures which is best obtained by direct measure. So much for the perpendicular position; let us now look at the horizontal, and consider whether it is better to fix the position of the front of scye by the back or front of the garment. Though we acknowledge the back to be the fixed part of the garment, we still give decided preference to those plans which fix it from the front, inasmuch as the width across the chest can be most easily and accurately determined, and is not affected by any variations in the allowance for ease, making up, and so on; and although the method of fixing the front of scye at two-thirds the scale may, and undoubtedly

does, produce garments remarkably near the mark, yet it is not so simple and reliable as the other plan. This also applies to measures taken from the back to the front of scye, which, passing over so many seams, wadding, &c., is quite likely to mislead us. Hence our preference for the plan of locating the front of scye by measuring across from the back to the front, half the chest measure and that allowance for making, ease, &c., our judgment dictates, and then measuring back from the front the across chest measure. In this way allowance is given for ease and making where it is needed, as nearly all the seams in a coat are between back and front of scye, and the ease is also located in the scye section, a plan which will meet the approval of the majority of our customers.

The Balance

Comes next, and is undoubtedly one of the most important principles connected with coat cutting. It is one on which a lengthy treatise of itself might be written, but we must refrain from doing more than examining so much of it as is necessary for the purpose of this work. Balance consists of the relative lengths of front and back, a good, evenly-balanced coat being generally considered as one with the front the same distance from the level of the bottom of scye upwards, as the back is from level of scye, and the width of back neck fixed at one-sixth. This may be counteracted by the lower part of the body of coat, for if the suppressions of the waist at the side are made in excess of the requirements of the figure, they have a very similar effect to that produced by shortening the shoulder. But assuming that the waist suppressions are in accordance with the requirements of the figure, then balance resolves itself into the relative length of back and front shoulder from the level of scye upwards.

As no garment can be said to fit well which is not well balanced, it behooves us to give this matter the most careful consideration. The coat with the long front shoulder will hang away behind, as if it had no connection with the person wearing it; whilst the one with a too short front shoulder will be all alive in the back, and cling to the waist with the utmost pertinacity. There is no doubt that the plan of finding the balance by measuring from the nape to a point two-fifths of the waist measure from centre of back on natural waistline, and then taking a measure from the nape of neck on a straight line, and again over the shoulder, is a thoroughly good one. It is not so easy in its application, as by taking the depth of scye, and length of front shoulder, which can both be applied in a most simple and expeditious manner. Hence our preference for dealing with the balance from the bottom of scye upwards.

The Waist Suppression.

This is a somewhat difficult point. We have never yet seen a satisfactory plan of obtaining the correct quantity of waist suppression in such a simple and practical method as to commend itself to the mind of the cutter in daily practice. In dealing with suppressions at any part, it is always necessary to remember that to suppress at one part means to produce fulness at another. The principles on which the waist suppression must be based, is to provide a receptacle for the prominences of the body. In making the suppression between back and sidebody, the chief aim is to provide a sufficient receptacle for the blades to allow of the coat going naturally into the hollow of the waist. If this is not done sufficiently, there is a fulness produced directly above and below the blades, causing the coat to stand away

at the waist, and to be full at the top of sideseam. The reverse would be the case if the suppressions were too much, and a fulness over the blades be produced. This, then, is the principle of waist suppression, and as long as it is done with due regard to the proportion of the figure, it will have no effect on any other part; but as soon as it is done in excessive or insufficient quantities, then it produces results on the lower part of the coat, the same as variation in the balance or length of the shoulder. Our plan, then, for body coats, may be gathered from the various diagrams in this work, and consists in taking out 1 inch between the line by which all the lines are squared across, to back seam at waist. This has the effect of lengthening the back balance and making the coat to fit close to the waist behind; then about 1½ inches between back and sidebody, varying according to the flatness or prominence of the blades, and about 1 inch between sidebody and forepart at waist under arm, for a proportionate figure (say 4 inches smaller at waist than chest). We have given all these quantities "about"; as fixing these by judgment, is decidedly the best plan. It is highly necessary they should be varied, to meet the requirements of different customers; and we trust our readers will be able to form such judgment for themselves, after perusing the general plan or principles upon which it is based. The next point for consideration is

The Spring over the Hips and Seat.

Much that has been said in dealing with the waist suppression applies with equal force to this. Our plan to get the run over the seat, is to square down from the fashion-waist 9 inches, to spring out from 1 to 1½ inches more or less, as the seat is more or less prominent, and to hollow out the waist between skirt and forepart and sidebody, so that a ¼ inch only of daylight or space shows between them for a close-fitting skirt. This must be carefully noted, as if this space is increased, so must also the spring over the seat, by at least double the quantity, when the extra width put into the skirt by this means will form a fold of drapery at the sides. If this last point is especially noted, many of the existing troubles in connection with skirts will disappear. The amount of fulness over the hips is generally fixed at about 1 inch, but it should always be borne in mind that figures which are thin at waist and prominent in the hips require more, and the reverse for stout waists. If pockets are to be placed at side, a still greater quantity is necessary. These, we believe, are the principal features to be noted in connection with this section, in order to produce satisfactory results. We are treating of the systems for skirts in another page.

Allowance for Making, Ease, &c.,

Comes next, and are matters upon which judgment must be exercised. The amount allowed must be decided first by the substance or thickness of the material, and next by the amount of ease required by the customer; for whilst one man will have a coat quite loose, another will require it to fit him as close as a glove. The customer's special requirements we must note when measuring him — putting a larger measure in our order book if a loose-fitting garment is required, and smaller if a close-fitting one, and so on; it being very easy when you have the tape round your customer's chest to ask him: "Do you like it easy-fitting, sir?" and adjusting the tape to meet his views, so that in cutting we only have to deal with the material. If this is very thin, 1¾ inches will be sufficient allowance; if medium, from 2 to 2¼; but if of

an exceptionally thick nature, 2½ or even 3 inches will not prove too much. It is just at this point that many garments are made unsatisfactory. A pattern has been used which has proved successful on previous occasions, without making any allowance for the difference in substance between a thin worsted and a heavy Winter Cheviot; consequently the garment is returned and the cutter looks upon the matter as a mystery; for the customer tells him this is as much a failure as the last was a success. Hence it is always advisable to remark on the pattern or, better still, fasten a piece of the material to it, carefully noting all details by which the last garment was made and success attained. This shows, we think, how these and all such matters should be carefully studied, since it is by the combination of these apparent trifles that success in cutting can be achieved.

The Location of the Neck Point.

It is quite needless that we should refer to the many controversies which have taken place in connection with this vexed question; to do so, would take up far more space than would be profitable to our readers. We will, therefore, at once proceed to express our own views on this topic, in as clear and lucid a manner as possible. It appears to us that the point should be directly influenced by the diameter of the neck and the degree of prominence of the chest. As we know there are many figures who have a very broad and flat front, although very thin through from back to front, the width across the chest is a good guide to define whether the man is broad and flat or the reverse. Consequently, we locate this neck-point by casting two segments — the one from the front of scye and the other from the front of chest — using the front shoulder as taken on the figure, less the width of back neck,

by which to sweep from the front of scye. Add 1 inch (more or less) to this quantity, to sweep from the front of chest, and then fix the position of the neck-point at the spot where these two segments intersect each other. We have worked by this measure for a lengthened period, and have found it a most satisfactory plan, as it produces a more crooked cut for the wide-chested and shoulders-backward figure than for the stooping and narrow-chested — a result generally admitted to be correct, and in accordance with the requirements of such figures. It may be as well, perhaps, to note, whilst on this topic, that when the neck-point is located in a backward position. it may be nullified either by cuts in the neck and forepart, or by well drawing in the front edge by stay tape, with a little difference in the result. The principle of this is, that the forepart that is originally cut crooked and then reduced to the normal by means of fishes and cuts in the neck and front, or by working up the front edge, would fit much closer to the front of scye and give a rounder breast worked up in the garment. It is, doubtless, a question to some minds as to which really produces the best fitting and most stylish garment, and one that might well form the subject of a profitable discussion, if only for the sake of bringing out the different methods of manipulation. We are inclined to think that if two coats were submitted for competition, the one cut with little or none added to the front shoulder when casting the second segment, so that any "slop-worker" might make it; and the other with say 1½ or 2 inches added, such as would require, and in fact must have, a careful manipulation of the front and a nice round produced on the chest — the latter would carry away the palm for artistic effect and general superiority of fit. Whilst acknowledging this, we yet feel there is a serious

difficulty in getting workmen to carry out such views in an efficient manner, and for that reason it is generally looked upon as advisable to err rather on the side of a straight than a crooked cut. The plan we are here advocating will be found in accordance with this view, for in practice we have seldom found it advisable to straighten the shoulder, yet we have, on one or two occasions, crookened it with advantage.

Having now got a good idea of what are the component parts of the Coat, and having examined in each Coat the most advisable measures, we find they are as follows: — (1) Chest. (2) Waist. (3) Depth of scye on back. (4) Lengths to natural and fashion waist. (5) Full length. (6) Style-width of back. (7) On to elbow and hand. (8) Width across chest. (9) Front shoulder. (10) Over shoulder. And, if thought desirable, the seat. Of course these measures may be supplemented by any that may suggest themselves to the cutter as likely to be of service to him in carrying out the customer's whims; as, for instance, supposing the gentleman desires an extra large sleeve, by far the best way would be to take the size of the elbow and hand, which will at once give you a good idea at the time of cutting.

In Measuring,

Always go about it in a business-like and methodical manner. Have your plan of taking the measures clearly defined before you commence, as nothing is worse than for the customer to notice hesitation on the cutter's part, as if he were thinking — "Let me see, which is the next measure?" It will be better for the inexperienced to carefully practice whatever system of measuring he decides upon adopting, on his friends, and so get at home with the tape, and overcome that nervousness experienced by many at first. We will assume, then, the above plan has been decided upon, and the customer is waiting to be measured, the material and style has been selected, and all the details entered in the order book. The cutter first takes the chest measure, which should be taken to agree with the customer's wishes, hence it is our invariable custom to ask, when taking this, "Do you like a close or easy fit?" when they will generally say, "That is too tight," or, "I like it pretty close", and so on; and by getting a knowledge of his views you are better able to produce a garment in accordance with his ideal. Now ask the gent to button his coat and then put the tape over both shoulders, down in front of the arms, bringing it back to the centre of back and keeping it close up to the bottom of the scye, at the same time using every care that the tape is not brought too high up in the centre. Now make a slight chalk mark at the centre of back, B, Fig. 1, and then proceed to measure, calling out each in order as taken. They should be entered in the order book by the clerk, who calls them back after you, so as to avoid mistakes, in the following order: — Depth of

FIG. 1.

FIG. 2.

scye, A B; natural waist, A to the hollow of waist, on to fashion-waist (usually about 2 inches lower) and then on to full length; and on this the customer's taste should be carefully consulted. Next, width of back with arm at side; then raise the arm, bring it forward and bend it, so that the wrist is opposite the centre of the front of the figure, and continue the measure from centre of back on to elbow and then to cuff. Again, consulting your customer's views as regards the length of sleeve — if he has no particular taste, measure to the wrist-bone.

Now measure across chest, E to E, Figure 2. Then take the front shoulder from A, Figure 1, to D of Figure 2. D is the level of the armpit, and may be got by putting the finger under the arm and measuring down to the top of the finger — or a pencil could be used in the same way. Now take the over shoulder measure from B over the shoulder at C and down to D both these latter measures should be taken closely. In measuring, it is always advisable to carefully watch for any abnormality, such as "one side lower than the other", "head very forward and back round, "prominent blades", and so on. Now is the cutters opportunity, and it depends very much on the skill and perception, as well as the capacity, to grasp your customer's wishes at this period that paves the way for after success. So our advice is, use your eyes as well as your tape, and enter the smallest detail in your order book that is likely in any way to aid you; leave nothing to memory, for it is sure to fail you.

As many may have to work from others' measures, we give a scale of measures from 24 to 50 breast, arranged not so much with view of proportion as the result of practical experience: —

			Lounge		Morning Coat						
Chest	Waist	Scye Depth	Nat. Waist	Length	Fas. Waist	Length	Across Chest	Across Chest	Across Chest	Front Shoulder	Over Shoulder
24	24	6¼	11¾	20			5⅛	19½	5¼	9½	12¾
26	25	6¾	13	22			5½	22½	5¾	10	13⅝
28	26	7¼	14	24			5⅞	25	6¼	10½	14¼
30	27	7¾	15	26			6⅛	27½	6¾	11	14¾
32	28	8¼	16	28	18	31½	6½	30	7¼	11½	15½
34	30	8⅝	16½	28½	18½	32	6⅞	31	7⅝	12	16¼
36	32	9	17	29	19	32½	7¼	32	8	12½	17
38	34	9⅜	17¼	29½	19¼	33	7⅝	33	8½	13	17¾
40	37	9¾	17¾	30	19¾	33½	8	33½	9	13½	18½
42	39½	10⅛	18	30½	20	34	8⅜	33½	9½	14	19¼
44	42	10½	18¼	31	20¼	34	8¾	34	10	14½	20
46	46	10¾	18½	31½	20½	34½	9	34	10½	15¼	21
48	50	11	18½	32	20½	34½	9¼	34	11	16	22
50	54	11¼	18½	32	20½	35	9½	34	11½	16¾	23

The application of these measures is as follows: —

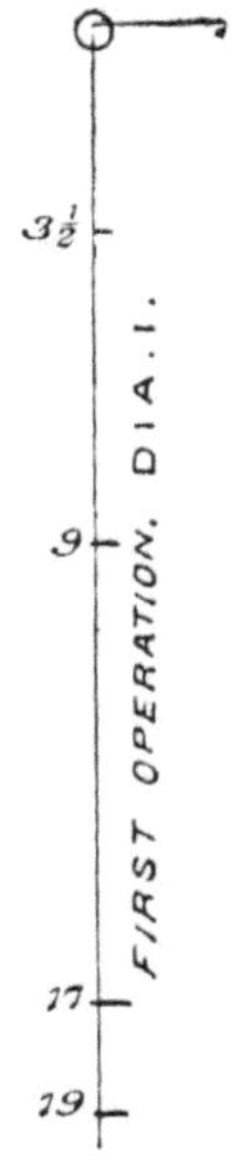

First Operation. Diagram 1.

Draw lines running at right angles to O, the one about 3 inches long and the other about 20. Come down from O to 3½, one-third of the depth of scye, plus ½ inch — this is really a matter of taste, and this rule is merely given as a good guide. O to 9 is the depth of scye; O to 17 is natural waist length, and O to 19 fashion waist length.

Second Operation. Diagram 2.

Draw lines at right angles to the various stations previously found. Come in 1 inch at natural waist 17, and draw back seam from O to 1, and then mark off the various widths on the various lines; from O to 2½ is one-twelfth breast, minus ½ inch; from back seam at 3½ to 7¼ is the width of back, plus 2 seams; from back seam on line 9 mark off to 20 the half-chest measure, plus

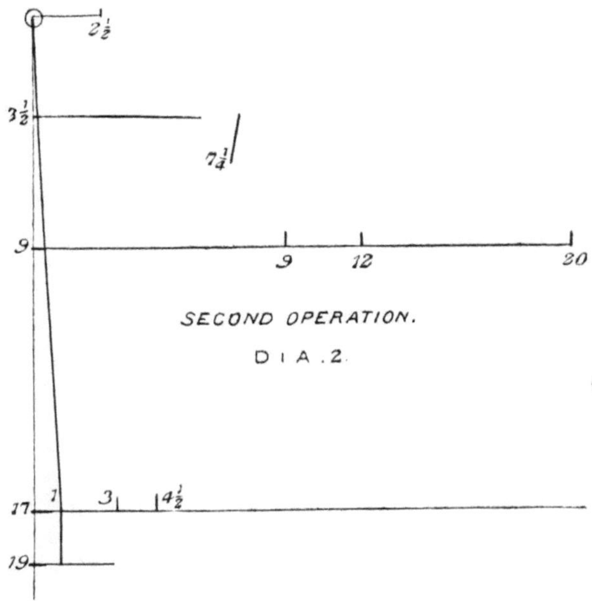

2 inches; back seam to 9 is ¼ breast; point 12 is found by measuring back from 20 the across chest measure; from 1 to 3, on line 17, is one-eighteenth breast measure, and 3 to 4½ is 1½ inches.

Third Operation. Diagram 3.

Come up from 2½ ¾ inch and shape back neck; draw shoulder seam from ¾ to C and hollow it slightly between ¾ and W; make C B the same as 1 3, viz., one-eighteenth breast; draw line from B to 17 and hollow sideseam of back ¾ inch and complete back.

Then draw sidebody, advancing from B a trifle, now, using point B to sweep for the bottom of sidebody, square down from 9 and hollow sideseam of forepart and sidebody ½ inch on either side, as at 8½ to 9½. The waist may then be measured up from 1 to 3, 4½ to 8½, and 9½ to 21½, allowing the same amount over the half waist measure as was allowed at the chest. We now proceed with the front shoulder, which is found by a series of sweeps.

Measure O to ¾ of back, deduct it from the front shoulder measure and by the remainder sweep from point 12 in the direction indicated by first sweep F. Now add 1 inch to this quantity (this is for an ordinary figure) and sweep again from point 20, as indicated by second sweep point F, and where these segments intersect each other locates the neck point. For the third sweep measure from A to W of the back and deduct it from the over-

shoulder measure; and, by the remainder, sweep from point 12, putting the finger on the tape at 1½ inches above this, so that the actual pivot would be 1½ inches above point 12; and then make the third sweep at D. From F to D is ¼ inch less than ¾ C of the back. This leads on to the

Fourth Operation. Dia 4.

Draft the shoulder seam, from F to D, slightly round — a very good plan is to draw a straight line from F to D and add about ½ inch of round at about two-thirds across the seam from F. Now shape the scye, from D to G, letting it touch the line at G 1½ inches up from 12 and at E, which is also 1½ inches from 12; let it be well hollowed at H; a good plan is to measure across from the angle at 12, ¾ inch. Let the back scye, between E and B, be kept close up. It will be noticed there is a little taken out between the back and sidebody, at B; this should

THIRD OPERATION
DIA. 3.

FOURTH OPERATION.
DIA. 4.

be about ¼ inch. We now come to the

Fifth Operation. Diagram 5.

Measure out, from F to V, one-twelfth breast, less ½ inch, or, if you have the neck measure, take ⅙ of the entire neck; from V to I is the same a-mount. Now draw breast line from V to 20 through 21½ to G. Line H G is got by squaring across from the bottom of side-body at right-angles to line O 19. The draft of

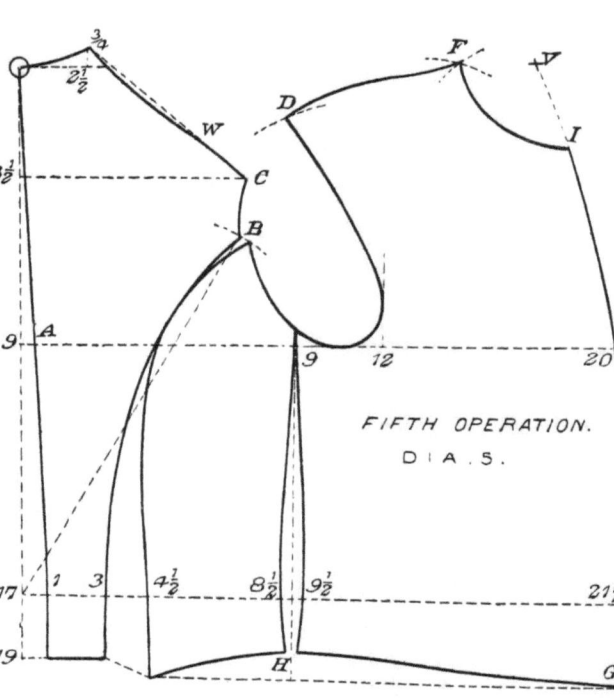

FIFTH OPERATION.
DIA. 5.

the body part may now be completed by hol-lowing the waist at H, about 1 inch. This completes the system for the body part, the application of which to the va-rious Body Coats will be explained further on.

Sixth Operation. Skirts.

We now pro-ceed to draft the Skirt, and, as will be seen by the diagram, we have illustrated all styles, as by so doing it will great-ly facilitate mat-ters when we come

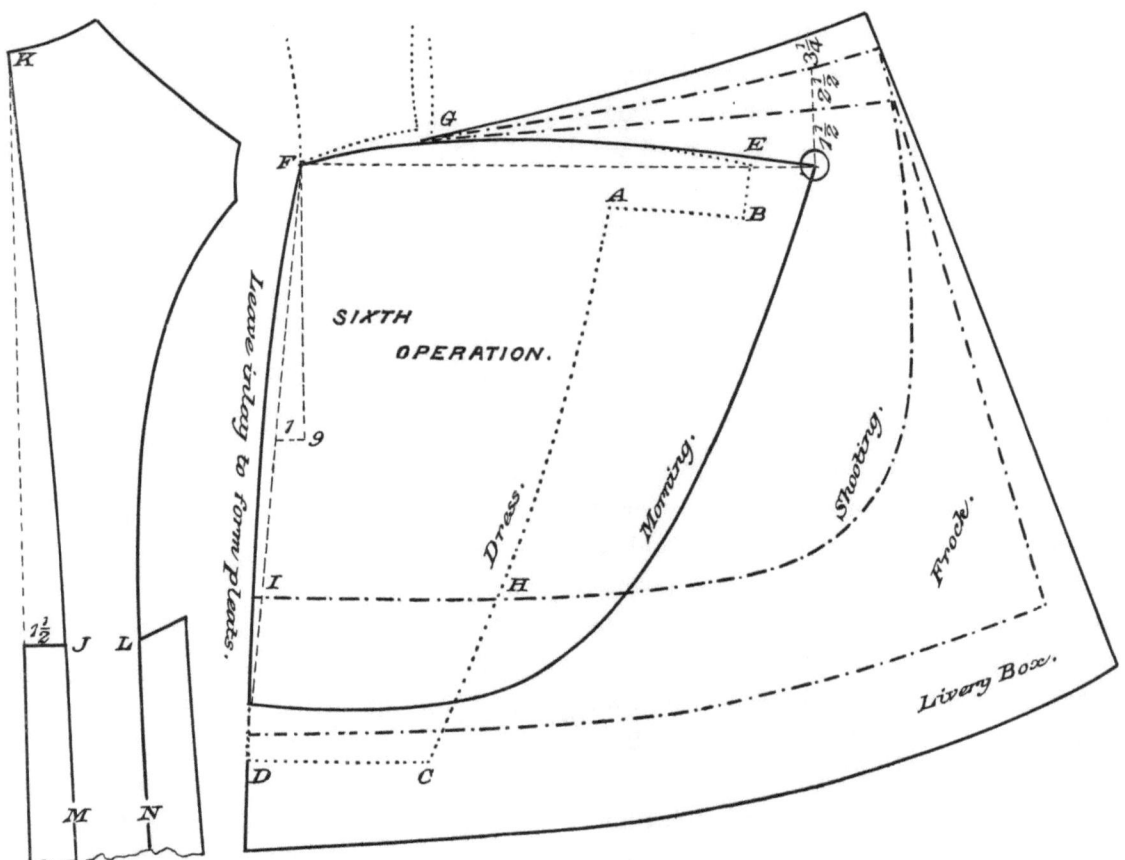

SIXTH OPERATION.

Leave inlay to form pleats.

Dress.

Morning.

Shooting.

Frock.

Livery Box.

to each garment, as well as make it quite plain to our readers. The system is as follows: — Square lines O F 9: O F is parallel with the line drawn through natural waist in previous diagrams of the body part, the top edge should be rounded as much as the forepart and sidebody is hollowed, less ¼ inch, and about 1 inch allowed for fulness; now square down to 9, 9 inches; come out from 9, 1 inch; and draw line from F through I to D, as shown, and round over the prominence of seat ½ inch. This may, of course, be increased if the seat is very prominent, but, as a general rule, this is thoroughly practical and safe. It will be noticed that no difference is made in any of these Skirts in that part which is bounded by G F D — that part requiring to fit the same in even such extreme styles as a Livery Greatcoat and a gentleman's Dress Coat — the only variation required is in the amount of crinoline or drapery at the sides; for it will be readily perceived that the fronts of all kinds of Skirts must run in harmony with the forepart, hence the alterations illustrated in this Diagram 6 are done with the view of producing varying degrees of fulness in the different styles.

The Morning Coat Skirt.

The run of the Morning Coat Skirt is quite a matter of taste, some liking them cut away very sharply, whilst others consider the style shown as the best taste, and as avoiding those extremes of style which always make a garment conspicuous. In making up, it is advisable to put a facing down the front and to leave a good plait in the lining over the hip, putting that part from F to G on quite plain, and nicely distributing the fulness from G to a point just above A, and so landing the fulness over the hip. The round opposite 1 should also be worked forward on to the hips.

The Dress Coat Skirt

As shown by dotted line is very little different in general outline from the Morning Coat, for, with the exception of the front being dropped a little at E, the top and back are the same. The length of the Skirt of a Dress Coat should be about 1 or 2 inches less than the fashion waist of a coat, such as, for instance, 19, 36. The width of the strap should be cut 1½ inches at E B and a trifle wide at A; the length from A to B should be one-third of the width from F to E and not including the width of lapel in either case, which comes to the end of the strap of a Dress Coat Skirt. The width of the bottom, from D to C, should be made about 1 inch less than half the distance from E to F, making this rather more in the smaller sizes and rather less in the larger sizes. These Skirts are generally lined throughout with the same cloth as the coat is made from, except when silk is desired, which is lighter, and more striking. The pockets are generally put in plaits, and are not unfrequently made from white silesia to prevent any possibility of the black soiling the white gloves which may be put in them. The front edge is usually slightly rounded; and we hear that the latest style in the West-End is to round away the corner, at C, in the style of a Morning Coat.

Skirt for Naval Uniforms,

Of both the Full Dress and Undress type, are of this class, with the exception that they are rather shorter, and the opening at waist or length of strap should be made one-fifth of the total size of waist, being fixed at that proportion by the official regulations published by the Admiralty.

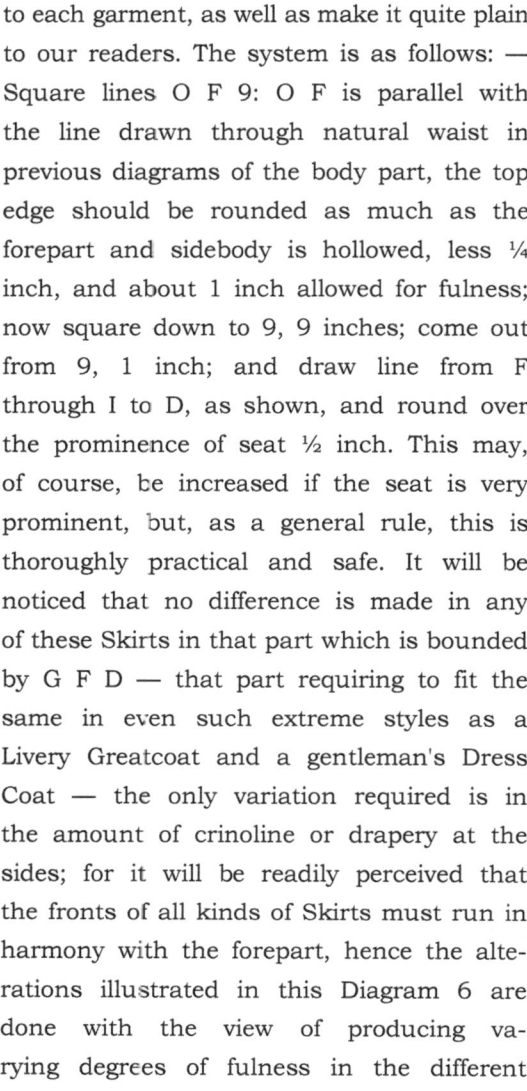

The Coatee Skirt

Is the same as for the Dress Coat, with the exception of being made shorter and heavier, being generally made to come just above the bend of the knee. The length may be taken on diagram, as at H I, and the strap should also be made a ¼ of-an-inch wider. A sword flap should be put on the centre of Skirt 11 inches long, pointed in the centre towards the back and with a point at top and bottom. Buttons are plugged through, opposite each point, and the Skirt is always lined through with cloth; but we shall refer to these later on. The next type of Skirt is

The Shooting Coat, or Gamekeeper's Skirt.

It will be readily perceived that as pockets are placed on the hips and plenty of fulness required in the skirt, more drapery must be allowed on in order to meet these requirements. We raise the front, at O, 1½ inches. Many people have an idea that it will affect the plaits, but such is a mistaken notion, for so long as no variation is made between G and F the skirts will fit the same; and the only difference in the fitting produced, by raising the front 1½ inches at O, will be to throw a fold of surplus cloth about the region of H. The front is generally kept very forward, the general outline being formed by the dot and dash line, and marked "shooting".

The Frock Skirt.

This includes Clerical, Gent's D.B. Frock, Coachman's, Groom's, Police Tunic, Fireman's ditto, Huntsman's Frock, and in fact any skirt of moderate length wanted to hang level in front and not too full at the sides. These skirts may be produced by coming up from O 2½ inches, and forming skirt seam, to nothing at G, and leaving

the part untouched behind that. There are two methods of getting a satisfactory run to the front. The one is by placing the forepart in a closing position and running the front of skirt in a continuous line with forepart; the other is to place one arm of the square on Fand come as much above 2½ as 2½ is above point O, and then drawing the front by the other arm. The length of front, side, and back should all agree, in order to get a satisfactory run to the bottom.

The Military Tunic Skirt

Is not required quite so full as this latter, still it is of the same stamp. Sufficient drapery, however, will be provided by drawing the top as described for the Shooting Coat, viz., coming up from O 1½ or 2 inches and giving a very little extra spring in front, and arranging the rest accordingly. The official regulations issued by the War Office state that the length of skirts for tunics shall be 9 or 10 inches, according to rank, for a man 5 feet 9 inches; and varying ⅛ inch for every inch in height.

The Livery Great Coat

And Top Frock is a very full skirt, and can be best produced by coming up from 3¼ to 3½ from point O, by which to get the run of waist seam and front edge. The length of these skirts varies as follows: — Groom's, well above the top boots, no flaps or pockets at waist; coachman's, to the middle of the top of top boots, with flaps and pockets at hips; footmen, longer still, reaching nearly to the ankle, with pockets in the pleats, and of course without flaps at the waist. It is always best to take these skirts from the crease edge of the material, or large wheel-pieces will be necessary, and as the above plan is quite as economical as any other, if not more so, it should be universally practiced, its advantages being apparent to the most unobservant eye. It is customary with these coats, as in fact all Frock Coats, to leave an inlay all down the front, which makes a nice edge, and forms a kind of facing to fell or stitch the lining to. It is hardly necessary for us to remark that Frock Coat skirts are invariably left plain round the bottom, *i.e.*, either with a raw or turned-in edge, but with no stitching or binding along that part; still, as these pages will doubtless be read by a good many novices, we note points which to the advanced cutter may appear superfluous. Our experience goes to prove that things of this sort are very valuable to young men, and help them to grasp the details of high-class tailoring more readily than they could if such points were omitted. The bottoms of the skirts of Morning Coats are frequently finished in the same way — the stitching on the edge terminating with the facing — but this is not an invariable rule, and in the case of bound edges the binding is always carried round the bottom. It only now remains for us to explain

The Back Skirts.

These are very simple, yet there should be a distinct method of arranging them, the most reliable plan being as follows: — Come out from J 1½ inches, and draw a line from K through this point as long as skirt is required. Square across from point 1½ by dotted line to L, and so make point L a trifle lower than J, and thus avoid the buttons coming above the back tack. Continue the back at J L down to M and N, leaving sufficient for the pleat beyond L N, and letting it point upwards at L — 1½ inch is a very good quantity. This should also be left on the back of all the skirts from F to D. In making up, the back skirts should be lined, and the lining put in slightly tight round the bottom edge, so as to make the skirts curl inwards. Many fancy this result can be obtained by stay tape being put up the back of plaits; such, however, is a mistake, as it is more than likely to cause them to curl outwards, so that the stay tape should only be put up the back skirts fair, or bad results will follow.

Seventh Operation. Sleeves.

There are few portions of a garment that give the cutter in daily practice more trouble than sleeves, for they must fit the scye, and be put in in the position intended, and at the same time the scye must be made to fit the wearer, or some special provision made in the sleeves for any deviation in the body part.

The Sleeve System. Diagram 7.

As we believe the safest plan on which any sleeve system can be worked is to take such measures from the scye as will enable us to produce a sleeve to fit and be in harmony with it, and, as the pitch or hang of sleeves has a very great effect on both their comfort and appearance, it will be necessary for us to clearly define where the seams should be pitched, so that the sleeves shall fit as we intended them.

We begin by measuring across from centre of back at C to front of scye at D, and deduct from it the width of back A to B; this remaining quantity agrees with O to 5 of Diagram 9. This can also be got by squaring up from the depth of scye line by the most backward part of the scye and measuring the distance between that line and the one in front. Now mark the pitch of the forearm seam, about ¾ of an inch above the level of bottom of scye. Now mark the pitch for the hindarm also to taste, say, at the sidebody seam. Then apply the square, with one arm resting on the back pitch and the other against the front pitch, and arrange the arm at E in the position it is desired the sleeve shall hang when finished; and whatever figure is opposite the front pitch at D should be used to find the top of hindarm, by measuring up, as from 5 to 1, and squaring across to 9. Now measure the distance between the two pitches, as from F to D, in a straight line, and measure across this distance, as

and better guide, make the width at elbow 1inch less than quarter-breast measure, and the cuff one-sixth of breast — making the quantities a trifle larger than the divisions given in the smaller sizes and a trifle smaller in the larger sizes. Hollow the forearm at elbow 1 inch, and then apply the width, as given above, from this hollowed part; bring the cuff to the line at bottom, and square the bottom from the

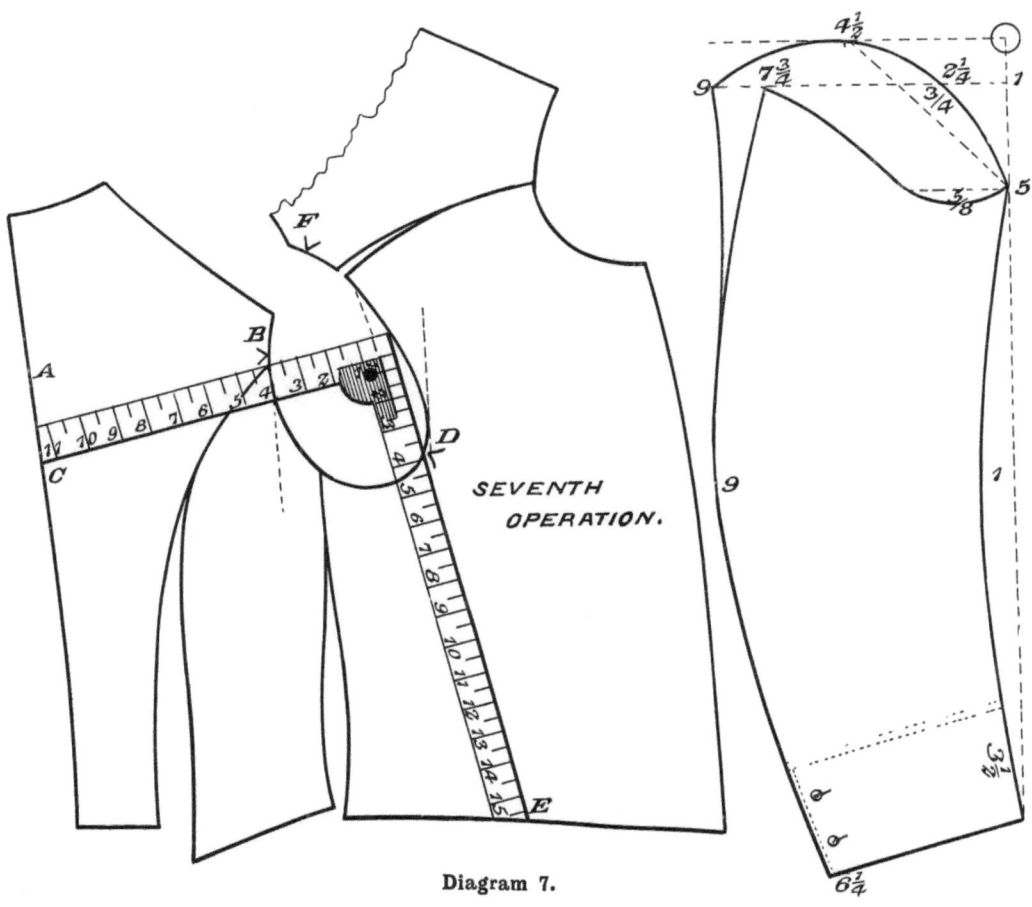

Diagram 7.

from 1 to 9; the round of the sleeve giving quite sufficient for fulness. Next divide this quantity in half, which finds point 4½; and half of this again gives point 2¼ on line 1 9. It now only remains to form sleeve head by points thus obtained. Now measure off the lengths of sleeve required, as per measures taken to elbow and wrist, and make the widths to taste or customer's wishes, which, in the absence of any other

elbow at 9 and wrist 6¼.

The Underside

Should now be marked by measuring round the scye between the two pitches, and applying this quantity across from 5 to 7¾; and, if the scye is intended to fit moderately close up to the figure, hollow the underside sleeve below the dotted lines at 5 a trifle less than the forearm pitch is above the bottom of scye, and then continue upwards to point 7¾, slightly rounding it as shown. This completes the system for the normal scye, and is as self-adjusting as most systems, allowing full scope for variations in the width of back; for, in the event of a narrower back being used, the depth of forearm is increased as well as the amount of fulness, both qualities which must commend themselves to every thoughtful cutter. But no sleeves will fit as clean and well as when the scye is cut to come just at the natural juncture of the arm and body.

Deviations for Abnormalities.

As many cutters have to cut from others measures we propose giving them a short list of the various abnormalities stating what additions or substractions to make from the sectional measures given in the scale on page 15 in order to adapt it to the special customer they are cutting for.

Although we have given definite quantities in every case, yet they can only be taken as illustrating the general principle, as the actual variation to make must always be in accordance with the degree of abnormality that exists in the customer, and which if the measures are taken as advised, will of themselves show that degree. At the same time it will prove a very useful lesson to those who take the measures as previously laid down, as it will show them several points where alterations should be made, which they would otherwise overlook, though these are really prepared to assist those who are cutting by the scale of proportionate sizes, and have not the opportunity to take their own measures.

Stooping. — Diagrams 8 and 9.

The stooping figure is longer and broader in the back and shorter and narrower in the front. The head and shoulders are more forward, and the blade bones are more prominent, whilst the arm hangs in a more forward position. This requires the back longer and broader and the front shorter and narrower, and the scye more forward.

These alterations will be met if we shorten front shoulder measure ¼ of an inch and add ¾ only instead of 1 inch to sweep for the neck point; and ½ an inch to the depth of scye, and take out a trifle more between back and sidebody at back scye; make the back a bare ¼ of an inch wider, and the front the same amount narrowed; do not give quite

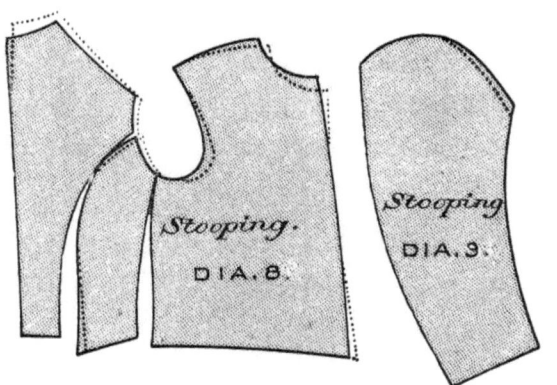

so much spring at bottom of sidebody and skirt, and make the sleeve more forward hanging, whilst the collar will require a shorter crease edge and therefore a relatively longer fall edge. It is not necessary to round the backseam, as it is preferable to take out more than usual between back and sidebody at top.

Erect. — Diagrams 10, and 11.

This figure has the opposite characteristics, generally speaking, of the stooping figure and may be met by the following alterations: Lengthen front shoulder ¼ inch and

22

add 1¼ instead of 1 to sweep for the neck point; shorten back ¼ inch add spring it out at the top of back neck of back seam a trifle; leave back and sidebody the same at top of sideseam, giving the preference to a little less suppression between back and sidebody at top of sideseam; make the back a bare ¼ of an inch narrower and the front a bare ¼ of an inch wider; give a a trifle more spring to the bottom of side-body and skirt, and make the sleeve to hang a trifle more backward, whilst the

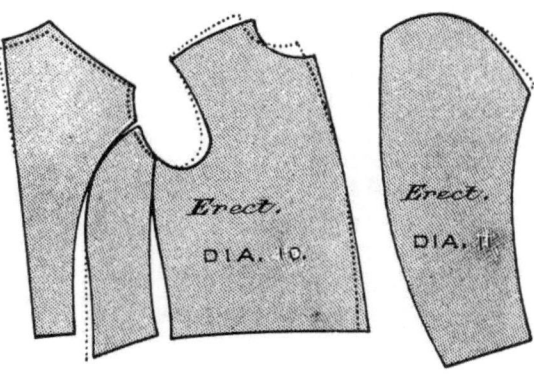

collar will require a shorter fall edge and longer crease edge than ordinarily; and in making up the front, the round should be carefully worked back over the prominence of nipple. It is really the extra promi-nence of the chest which necessitatès the sweeping of 1¼ more than front shoulder, instead of 1 inch, and not because extra lengths of front edge is needed for the erect figure. The 1¼ so added really amounts to a wedge let in across the front to provide room for the prominence of chest, and which, if the garment is to fit snug in the front, must be drawn in and shrunk away.

Corpulency. — Diagram 12.

Add on ⅓ of disproportion at under arm seam, and add the same amount and the length of forepart at front, and then round-ing it away at bottom. The remaining ⅔ goes on the front. It will always be as well to remember in dealing with corpulent figures, that they *generally*, but not always, carry their shoulders rather backward, are rather flat in the back, are somewhat erect or shorter in the back, as if to counter-balance the increase of size which takes place mostly in the front, whilst if the figure is at all short and the degree of corpulence great, it will be found they are short in neck. All these characteristic figures are provided for in the scale to be found on page 15, to the extent of the corpulency there given. But as

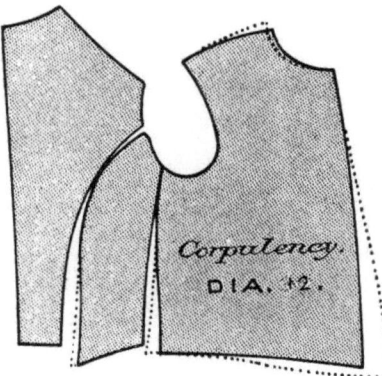

we can only give what we should expect to find under certain circumstances, it will be as well for everyone to take their measures on the customer, and then make provision for the corpulency as explained for Diagrams 76 and 77, as all the other points will be provided for in the measures taken on the customer.

Slender Waists, Diagram 13.

Reduce the size ½ at the underarm seam,

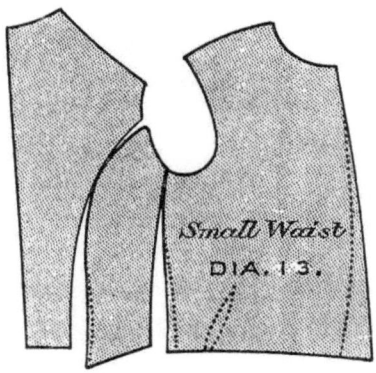

and take off the remaning ⅔ at the front, whilst it will be found advantageous to take out a fish at side of waist as shown.

Long Neck and Sloping Shoulders. — Diagram 14.

Add ¼, ⅜, or ½ an inch (according to the extent of the abnormality) to the front shoulder measure, and the depth of scye,

leaving the over shoulder the same, whilst ¾ will be better than 1 inch to sweep for the neck point from the front edge.

Short Neck and Square Shoulders, Diagram 15.

Reverse the above alterations, viz., shorten the depth of scye and the front

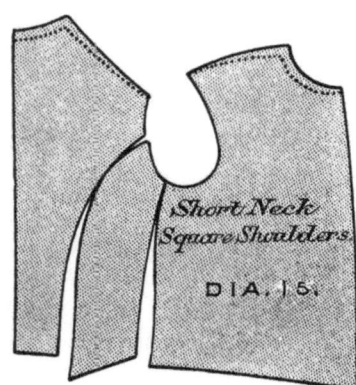

shoulder, leave the over shoulder the same, whilst the amount should be 1¼ rather than 1 inch to sweep for the neck point.

Forward Shoulders. — Diagram 16.

Reduce the width across chest a trifle,

say ¼ or ⅜, and add to the width of back the same amount.

Backward Shoulders. — Diagram 17.

Increase the width across chest, and

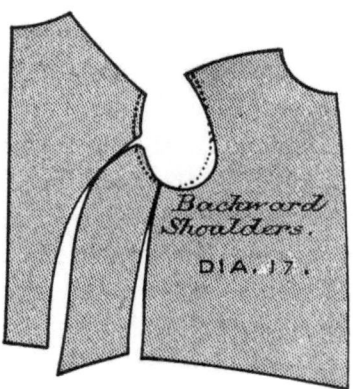

reduce the width of back, being the reverse of the above alteration.

Prominent Blades. — Diagram 18.

Take out more between back and side-

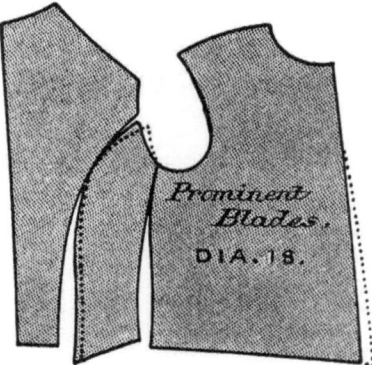

body at both top and bottom, say ¼ at top, and ⅜ at bottom on waist line.

Flat Blades. — Diagram 19.

Take out less between back and sidebody,

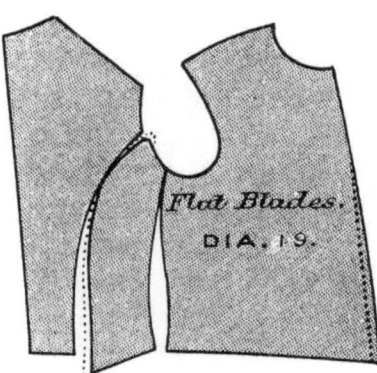

say ⅛ less at top and ¼ less at bottom.

Very Hollow at Waist, a kind of bending backwards. — Diagram 20.

Come in more from construction line at

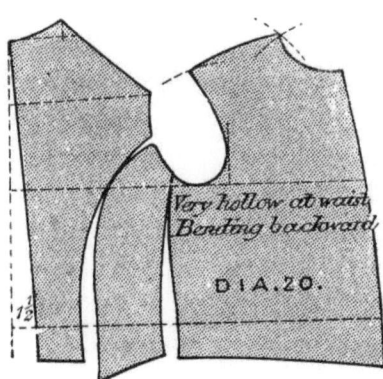

natural waist to back, say 1¼ or 1½ instead of 1 inch.

Very Flat at Waist. — Diagram 21.

Come in less from construction line at

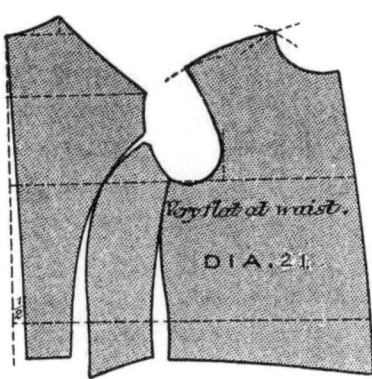

waist to back seam, say ½ or ¾ instead of 1 inch,

Short Waists. — Diagram 22.

As a general rule, it will be found that a person short-waisted will also be square on the shoulders, but not necessarily so; still it will be advisable to make the garment a trifle squarer in the shoulders or shorter in

the neck for persons of this type. The alterations we recommend for this figure would be to shorten the depth of scye and front shoulder ⅙ of an inch for every inch the customer is short in the waist, whilst the measures will naturally work out the garment shorter in the body and bring the spring for the hips higher.

Long Waists. — Diagram 23.

The reverse of the above will generally be found correct, viz., lengthen the depth

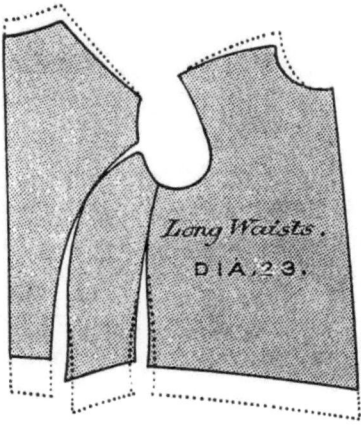

of scye on the back and the front shoulder measures ⅙ of the extent the figure is long in the waist, but as we have before stated, this does not necessarily follow, and the cutter must use his judgment, if he does not take the full set of measures to help him in this direction.

To produce Ease in the Scye.

If the shoulders are only large, it will generally be found sufficient to deepen the scye ¼ and advance the scye ¼, diagram 24;

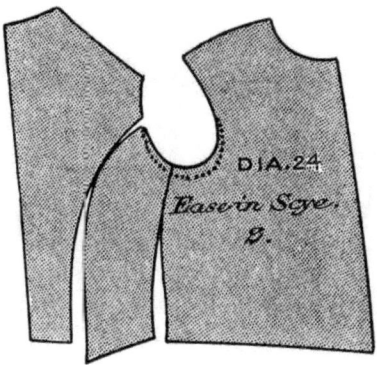

but if the customer has a great objection to the scye touching him at all, add ½ an inch to the over-shoulder measure, ¼ of an inch

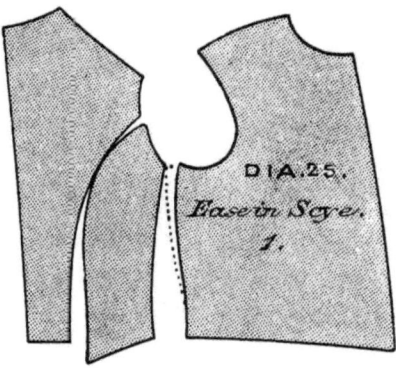

to the front shoulder, and sweep by ¾ instead of 1 inch, diagram 27. This will be found to produce the same effect as if a wedge had been inserted in the front of scye. Tightness in the scye arises from three principal causes: 1st. — Insufficient distance from the centre of back to the front of scye, diagram 25. 2nd. — Insufficient distance from the nape of neck to the bottom of scye, diagram 24. 3rd. — The scye being too

small in circumference for the arm, such as would be produced if the scye points of shoulders were too low and the two above correct, diagram 26. So that in producing a remedy it will be necessary to find the

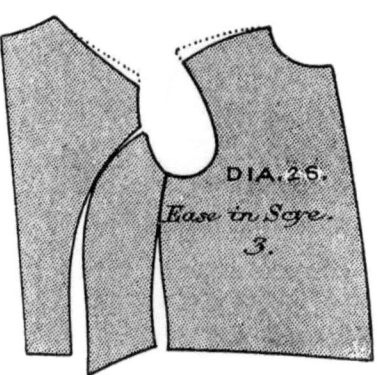

cause of the evil and remedy accordingly, whilst the method we have given above, and illustrated on diagram 27, should only be adopted when all the others have failed, as it will produce a fold across the chest from the front of scye, and consequently will not

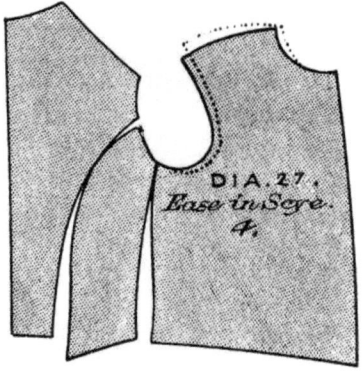

fit; still it is very useful for a special purpose, for there are a large number of customers who care very much more for ease at this particular part than style or appearance. We treat more fully of these abnormalities further on, but give here a brief *resumé*, so that students of these articles may know the deviations to make in cutting by taking the proportionate measures for the breast as given in the scale.

LAPELS. — PLATE 1.

These adjuncts to a coat may be described as that part which is added to the front of the coat beyond its actual centre, which would only allow the garment to fasten with hooks and eyes; hence all garments that do not fasten in that way have lapels to them. Laples may be divided into two parts, viz., those that are cut on the forepart and growing to it, and those that are cut off. It is with the latter we shall deal with more particularly. A few remarks however connected with the former ought not to be omitted. It is always well to remember that the front edge of any coat should be either originally cut, or so manipulated by the workman as to be quite straight, and any round that is added should be carefully worked back on to the breast; hence in order to get a nice roundness at that part, many cut their coats with a long and round front edge, which has to be worked up with the view of producing an effect, so that whatever style of front is adopted, it will be necessary to adapt the lapel to it, and, if need be, take out a cut as is usual with D.B.'s, or a great deal of surplus length will show itself on the outer edge; and in the adjustment of this lies the whole art of cutting lapels. But to this we shall refer presently in showing the practical application to the diagrams.

Dress Coat Lapel. — Diagram 29.

This shows the style of lapel more generally used in the provinces, and may be looked upon more as an illustration of style than embodying a system; the silk facing is brought to the end of the holes, there being usually 3 in the lapel, the top one running with the end of lapel. The great point, of course, in connection with this is to get it stylish and smart and avoid any tendency to a heavy appearance. The collar might, if anything, be brought lower with advantage; as will be noticed, it is made to turn very low, the fourth hole being consequently omitted.

Diagrams 31 and 34

Show how this is cut, and, as will be seen, the sewing-to edge is cut almost straight, ¾ of an inch being hollowed, which is done with the view of giving sufficient on the outer edge to lie nicely on the breast; for present, style the widths at the various parts are as follows: 1¼ or 1½ at bottom, 2½ or 2¾ at the widest part, and 2½ at top, measuring in a slanting direction. The length is obtained by measuring the length of forepart and strap of skirt as shown in diagram 29, and shortening the lapel a good ¾ inch. In order to get a nice clean edge, it is always advisable to cut it in the manner shown in diagram 34, which is arranged with the lower part cut on the crease, the dotted line showing the actual size of the lapel; the large V shown at top is stoated up; as it is arranged to come just on one side it does not show, and the edge is thus very much thinner than could be arranged in any other way; this is of great value when the edges are corded and stitched behind, as is so popular at present when worsted material is used, as it renders the putting on of the cord and stitching very much easier than if the edge was thicker.

For Livery Coatees

This is very important, at least we once found it so to our cost, for it fell to our duty to turn a raw edge into a bluff one for this class of coat; in wear the raw edge had frayed out and looked anything but satisfactory. The style of lapel adopted for these is much the same as illustrated on diagram 29, only of course minus the silk breast facings, and to have three holes below and two above the turn, and cut rather heavier, *i.e.*, wider.

Roll Collar Dress Coat, Diagram 30.

It is difficult to say which is the part that is the most important in this style, the lapel or collar, for, paradoxical as it may seem, the lapel is made up principally of the collar. A reference to the diagram will readily explain our meaning. From which it will be gathered we cut these the same way as the old-fashioned Dress vests. The lapel seam in this case is of no other use than for style and to carry it to the bottom; so that it might just as well be cut on the forepart, in fact, it often is done so and the strap of skirt carried through to the front. Some contend it would be very much better to make all roll collar Dress coats single-breasted, claiming an advantage for this style in being able to fasten it at waist in putting on an overgarment; be that as it may, present fashion dictates D.B., with lapel seam and buttons on either side, and gentlemen are very slow to change; the distance M D is cut just long enough to allow the seam to come well above the turn. Our diagram illustrates the present style of facing, these with black Moiré, which is brought right to the edge. The collar is produced by the system given on page 29, so that it will be unnecessary for us to repeat the illustrations there given.

The Top Frock Lapel, Diagram 32.

As this coat buttons very high, it is necessary to allow extra length on the outer edge, to allow it to turn freely. The dotted line shows the straight line to which the forepart will have to come, the round being pressed back to the centre of breast; the top edge of lapel is sprung out about 1 inch at top, which will have the same effect as if a wedge had been let in the outer edge at at turn. The width of this may be made, 3 top, 3½ centre, and 2½ bottom. The bottom edge at waist seam, as will be seen, is cut to agree with that part, a point which must never be overlooked, or the waist seams will not come together when the garment is buttoned.

Diagram 35.

Shows a Frock coat lapel, suitable to button three. The dotted line is the straight line, and it has the sewing-to edge slightly rounded instead of hollow, and consequently there is less length on the outer edge, such not being necessary, as the coat does not turn so high. The two principles to be understood in lapel cuttings are: first, a round sewing to edge produces a short outer edge, and a hollow sewing to edge produces a long outer edge, second, a coat turning high requires more length than a coat rolling low, and *vice versa*. With these instructions, the cutter will be enabled to produce that style of lapel to meet the requirements of each coat. The width of a Frock coat lapel as worn at present, is 2¼ at top, 2½ to 3 at breast, and 2 to 2¼ at waist. Some like them heavier than others, but the heavier ones are not looked upon as being nearly as smart as the lighter ones. A good deal of variation in the style of a coat can be introduced by the run of the outer edge of the top of lapel; some firms keep them straight, while others approve of a decided round at that part.

The Livery Overcoat Lapel, Dia. 33.

All garments of this class which fasten right up to the throat, have the lapels cut exactly by forepart; the top is cut down in the opposite direction to that usually done. The reason for this is, the top button should always be arranged for the collar to just slip under it as shown in diagram; it is cut about 2¾ wide at top, and 2½ at bottom, and drawn straight between these two points. This same system applies to

Naval Full Dress Uniform.

Lapels, which are made with a stand collar and fastening to the throat, are not cut nearly so heavy as those just described, and are pointed up at top, the width begin about the same as for the Dress coat, diagram 31, and are cut on the same plan as described for diagram 33.

Hints in General.

In draughting any lapel that has a turn at all, it is always advisable to fold it back and chalk round it to see if the shape and style is the same as desired, as they frequently appear quite different when turned over and the collar put to it, to what they do when cut. Care should also be taken to get the collar ends to run in unison with the top of lapel, as many an otherwise good coat is spoiled by carelessness at this part. Those cutters who take a pride in their work and endeavour to infuse as much style in their coats as possible, are most particular about these points. We should do well to follow in their footsteps, as nothing in the shape of style looks worse than a lack of harmony between the various parts of a garment, and especially so when they occupy such a prominent position as do the lapels and collars of, say, a Frock coat.

COLLARS. — PLATE 2.
Diagrams 36 to 42.

It is quite unnecessary we should enter into an argument to show the important part a collar plays in the fit of a coat, as anyone who has had the least experience in tailoring knows that. There is one point, however, on which a little explanation may be, beneficial, and that is the reason why collars should always be put on slightly long in the hollow of the gorge. It is a generally acknowledged rule in tailoring, that all-round seams should be slightly fulled on, and all hollow ones held tight or strained out. The reason for this is, that as a circle increases or diminishes in diameter, so does the circumference vary, and as the seam taken off the gorge increases the length, so the seam taken off the collar decreases it, the circle in the former being enlarged and in the latter reduced; and in order to avoid the collar being in any degree tight, it must be put on long to allow for this natural consequence of seaming a round edge to a hollow one.

The Ordinary Coat Collar, Diagram 37.

The system we here give is one of the best known to the trade, and from practical experience we can confidently recommend it, as it is based on sound principles and requires only the smallest amount of manipulation. All collars of this class, as will be readily understood, consist of two parts, the stand and the fall, the stand consisting of that part which comes from the coat up a certain distance on the neck of the wearer. The neck of the coat — or what will be readily understood as the collar seam — is located to come to the 7th vertebrae of the spine, and the collar stand is usually made to come about 1¼ inches above that, more or less. The fall is fixed entirely to taste, and may be made wider or narrower according to fashion. For a morning coat or jacket, the present style depth is about 1¾, and it is to such dimensions the collar, as illustrated in diagram 37, is drawn.

This system is by no means a new one, but rather one of those old and tried friends which have proved so highly satisfactory as to render it unnecessary to seek a better. It answers all the requirements of an ever varying practice. The mode of drafting is as follows: — After fixing the height at which it is desired the coat shall turn, mark up from the hollow of the gorge a trifle less than the height of stand desired as at O, say 1 inch for 1¼ stand, and draw line M C through O; now come down from C to B the difference between the height of stand and depth of the fall, which in this case is ½ an inch only, and draw line from B to O; this finds the crease row or the part of the collar which comes to the top when the collar is finished; now come down from B to A the height of the stand required, and draw the sewing on edge of collar from A through the hollow of gorge part N, and allowing a trifle of overlap at D; now measure up from B to G the depth of fall and shape the collar end at F to the style desired, which is best done by turning the lapel back and marking round it on the forepart, the style of step deemed good taste. Great care should be exercised in this, as it is without doubt the most prominent feature in the coat when finished, and one that readily shows whether good or bad taste has been displayed in shaping it. Having marked up from D to F, draw G to F; the back should be placed at A, and the collar at A B made to run with it, the fall at G B being allowed sufficient spring for it to turn over nicely.

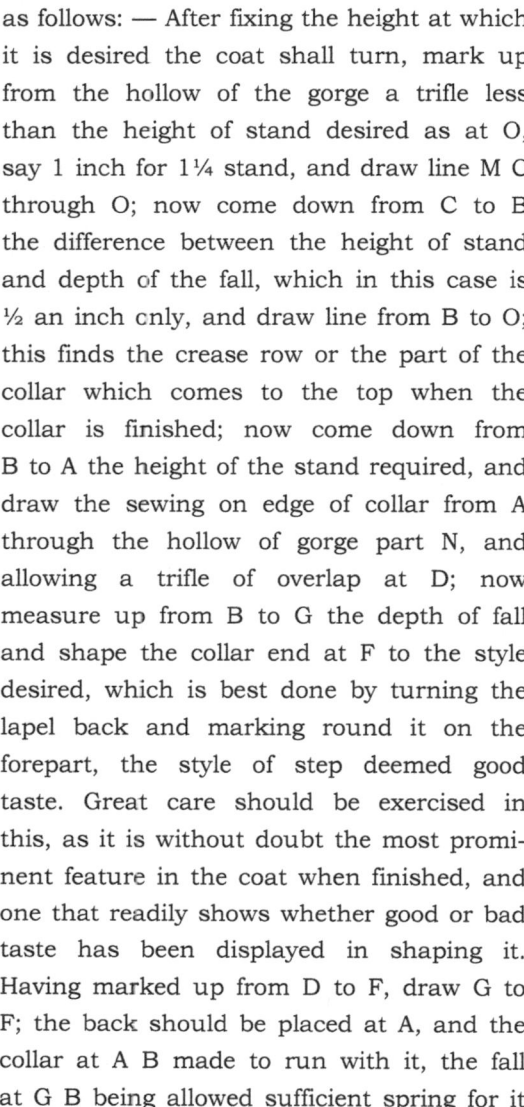

Overcoat Cape Collar, Diagram 38.

With the view of illustrating the adaptation of the system to a collar with a very heavy fall, we have prepared this diagram, as it shows in a very ready manner one of the principles of the system, viz., the deeper the fall the longer the fall edge becomes, a feature which will readily commend itself to the common sense of all; it is worked in precisely the same way as just described, so that it is quite unnecessary we should repeat, the various stations being marked with the same letters.

Dress Coat Collar, Diagram 41.

This shows its working for a coat rolling very low, and requiring what is known as a commanding collar. As will be seen, the fall edge of this is very much shorter than either of the others, a very essential part of any collar suitable for a Dress Coat. As a general rule it is always better to err on the side of a too long fall edge to a collar, but this is not in accordance with Dress Coat requirements, it being always necessary to keep it fairly short on the fall edge.

Sailor Collar, Diagram 42.

This collar is cut by putting the back and foreparts with the shoulders closed, L K being the back seam and the centre of the collar, K L is the width across the back, which may be regulated to taste; I is the the point at which it is desired to meet in the front. The collar can be raised according to taste in the details of shape, &c., but the principle of cutting them are as shown.

The Stand Collar. Diagram 40.

These collars which are put on garments to fasten up to the neck, may all be cut from one standard pattern, by varying the length at back and the height at top. The two styles generally used in this way are the stand collar and the Prussian collar. The system for cutting the former is as follows: Draw line A E, and mark off the length of collar desired; come up from E to D 1 or 1¼ inches, and round the sewing to edge from D to join the line A E about half-way; mark up from A to B the height desired at the back, and D to H the height desired in front, and draw top edge from H to B; the front at H is receded about ½ an inch from a line drawn at right angles to A E. The system for producing

The Prussian Collar Dia. 39.

Is as follows: Draw line A E the length of collar desired; come up from E to D 1 inch, and draw the sewing to edge from D to A, hollowing it to about half-way across from A to E. Mark the height of stand required, as from A to B, and draw the crease edge as shown, regulating the width of front to taste; the fall is then added below this, as at G F. This style of collar is frequently used for Clerical and Livery garments, especially for Livery Overcoats. These are generally lined in the stand and just on the edge of fall, wide enough to take the stitching, in which case the stand is cut the same as the stand collar, diagram 40. In dealing with Livery Overcoats it is always well to remember the gorge must be lowered a seam on the left side, or it will not button up to the neck in a clean manner.

The Collar Lining

Is best cut from the cross of the material, slightly on the bias, but on no account from the lengthways of the material, or the up and down. If there is a face to the cloth, the way of the "charlie" should be made to run down, as from G to A. The importance of this will soon be seen if the collar is folded over at the crease row, and the fall and stand rubbed between the finger and thumb, when the fall, having the pile running opposite to that of the stand, will keep it in position.

The Collar Canvas, Diagram 35.

Some may think this can be put in any way, but we hold it is highly essential it should be put in the way we are about to describe, if we wish to have both ends of the collar retain the same shape. The fine lines represent the threads of the canvas, and, as will be seen, it is joined in the centre, that being the only method of getting both ends of the collar to have the canvas the same; as will be seen, the threads run straight from N to P, and on the bias in all other parts. In stitching the stand, it should be remembered the purpose for which it is done is to impart a firmness or stiffness at that part, and that the padding in the fall is done with the view of making it curl inwards. We only point this out as we have seen many men do it apparently without any idea of what was its purpose, and to make it a custom of padding the stand as well as the fall.

Hints in General.

A stooping figure requires a longer fall edge and shorter crease row than the normal, whilst the erect requires a longer crease row and shorter fall edge. The stooping figure allows the collar being put on shorter, and the erect one longer, than the normal. A straight-cut shoulder requires a very long collar, and a crooked one will bear a rather short one if the shortness is put on in the right place; by shortness in this case, we mean less fulness than would be put on in a normal shoulder, but by no means contraction.

This, we think, pretty well exhausts the subject of collars from the cutter's point of view; and in drawing this subject to a close, we would repeat this as a very important item: always avoid a short collar, as it is more fruitful in producing defects than any other part of the coat and may be justly looked upon as the key to the garment.

Morning Coats. Diagram 28, Plate 3.

Probably there is no garment the present-day cutter is called upon to cut more frequently than the Morning Coat; it is undoubtedly the coat of the period, used the same for all occasions be they grave or gay. The funeral or the wedding is alike attended in the Morning Coat. There is great scope for varying it to suit the taste of all classes, not only in the height of buttoning, the run of the front, but even the length is subject to considerable variation; so much so, that there can scarcely be considered a correct length in the same sense as we should speak of the regulation for a Frock or Dress Coat. The young man, the old man, the business man, and the professional, all wear the Morning Coat, therefore little wonder that the styles are as varied as the classes who adopt them. From the costermonger who indulges in his "pearlies" and velvet corners to his pockets, to the prince with his neatly bound three-button Morning Coat, there is a very wide range, whilst all the intermediate styles are variations of this trifle or that detail, and so developing a special shape or fashion and almost making a distinct garment. Seeing, then, the wide popularity of these coats, we felt it was one of the most important garments dealt with in the "Guide", and one that we ought to give a special prominence to. To meet this effectually, the first thing to be done was to draw a diagram to the half inch scale, so as to convey to our readers a good embodiment of style in the various parts, every detail being brought out in the clearest possible manner; and in order that the holes and breast pocket should appear on the left forepart, we have reversed the diagram, preferring to draft towards rather than from us. We will now turn our attention to

The System. Diagram 77.

Commence by drawing line A B, A X; A to B is one-sixth neck, or, if you have no idea of the size of the neck, one-sixth

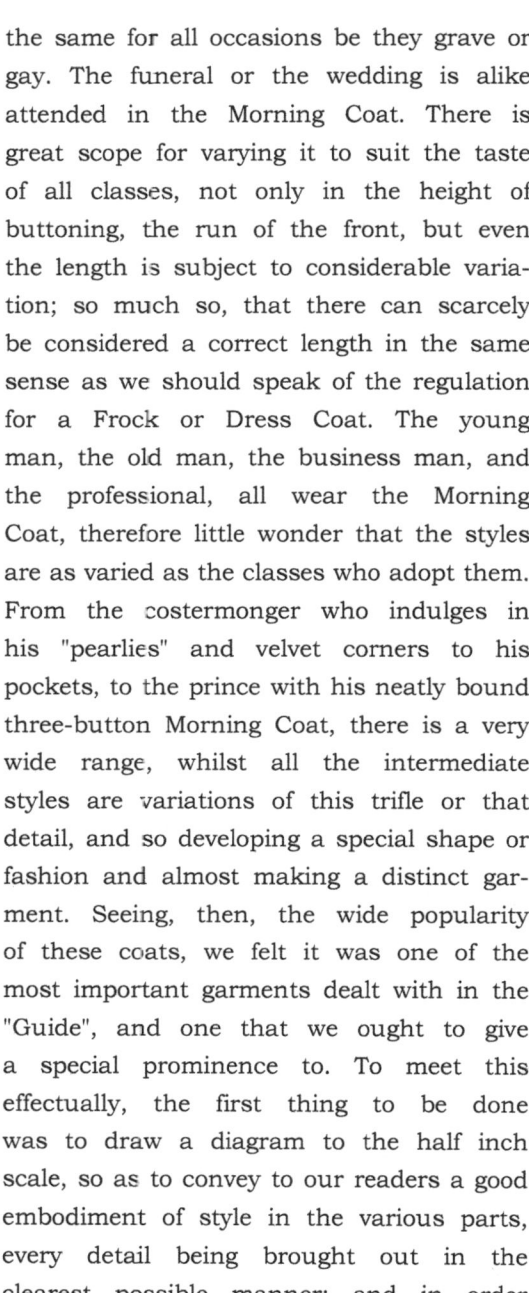

of the half breast will do, as it is really little more than a question of style, and any variation of this part would be adjusted in the forepart. Still, it is always advisable to produce garments harmonious in every detail if we possibly can, and we think that end can be best obtained by fixing A to B at one-sixth of the neck, which for this purpose may be fixed at one-sixth less than the half breast: thus 18, less one-sixth, 3, is 15, which would be about the size of neck for most men of 36 breast, at any rate near enough for our purpose here. Now raise point B one-fourth distance A to B above the straight dotted line, and draw the back neck; A to N is the depth of scye, 9; A to C is ½ inch more than one-third the depth of scye, but as this is a matter of taste, it may be raised or lowered without in any way affecting the fit, as its use is only to fix the shoulder seam slope. At present it is considered good taste to keep this rather high, as it gives a square-shouldered, military appearance, and at the same time apparently increases the length of waist. The division we have given is just a medium style, calculated to suit the majority, and devoid of those extremes which invariably do more to defeat good taste in a garment than to make it especially stylish. We merely mention this, as we have seen many coats cut in leading West-End firms, where the level of shoulder has been fixed at 1½ only down from A, and, needless to say, produced a very extreme garment. A to E is the natural waist length, and on to X the fashion length of waist. Now square across lines C M, N G, and E L, by line A X; come in from E to 17 from ½ to 1 inch, according as the customer is very hollow or flat in the back, and draw back seam as shown, slightly hollowing it at 9. The effect of coming in from E to 17 is really to lengthen the back balance — a feature experience has shown necessary with body coats, in order to get them to sit snug and close to the waist at the back, with figures at all hollow in the back. Now measure off the width of the back about 1 inch *below* the line C M, allowing two seams, when working from measures taken direct on your customer, but not when working from the scale, as they have already been added in it; now measure across from 9 to G on the depth of scye line, the half chest measure plus the allowance for ease, seams, &c. We have found 2 inches a good quantity for general purposes: this would make the distance from back seam at 9 to the breast line at G 20 inches. In allotting this amount for ease, &c., probably lies one of the great features of successful cutting, as we have not only to take into consideration the nature and substance of the material, but also our customer's idea of a fit, for some materials consume at least ½ an inch more in making than others. Moreover, what some gentlemen would call fit others would say was altogether too tight or too loose; and as our aim should always be to please our customers and cater for their wants, we must not — indeed, dare not — overlook this important factor in achieving the desired end.

Come back from G to H the across chest measure, 8 inches, which locates the front of scye, and find point I at 1¼ inches above this for all sizes; the width of the back scye, as from M to top of sideseam, is usually fixed at 2 inches, or one-ninth of the breast measure — rather less in the larger sizes; but this is another of those points wherein taste may be applied in dealing with the various types of this garment, in order to produce each style in perfect harmony with the remaining parts.

The sidebody seam of back may now be drawn. The experienced cutter invariably does this by "rock of eye"; but inasmuch as this work is to a large extent of an educational character, we give a method whereby extremes may be avoided, and which will produce the medium style which only requires plain working up. Draw a line from top of sideseam of back to E, on line A X, which, as will be seen, is at the natural waist, and come towards the back seam ¾ of an inch from this on line N G. This guide will enable the most unpractised to draw the seam in something like good taste and style.

The Sidebody.

The sidebody comes next. Take out ¼ of an inch at top and advance it a like amount, so that in making, the balance will not be disturbed; take out 1½ inches at J for all sizes, varying this in accordance with the prominence or flatness of the blades, generally increasing it for stooping figures and decreasing it for erect ones. Drop point R by sweeping across from bottom of sideseam of back, making the top of the sideseam the pivot; this extra length is necessary owing to the process of seaming, lengthening the back and shortening the sidebody, which can soon be proved by marking ¼ inch from the edge of each and measuring. The sidebody is now drawn nearly straight below line N G, the deviation being a little round just below the line N G, and curving into a slight hollow on waistline at J; draw a line across from R to S, squared by A X, and hollow bottom of waist seam at Q about 1 inch (another point of taste); from 9 to U is a quarter of the breast, from which draw a line at right angles to line N G, and take out half an inch on either side, and so find the width of sidebody and sideseam of forepart. In laying down these guides, we wish particularly to impress on everyone that they are by no means principles, as the position of the underarm

seam may be varied to taste or convenience; the mode we give being such as would produce medium styles, thus forming a good starting point for students to work from; at the same time it will be well to note that a narrow sidebody is generally considered to produce a better effect than a wide one. There is one point connected with the top of sidebody it is as well to note, and that is the shape at ⅝; it should always be the aim of every cutter to keep the back scye as close up to the figure as possible, as he is then able to hollow his under sleeve out more, without producing any drag, and at the same time getting the sleeve as clean-hanging as possible at this part, consistent with the provision for bringing the arms forward. As some may require a guide for this also, we give the following plan: Draw a line from M to U, and never hollow more than 1 inch, ¾ is preferable, and is the quantity to which the diagram is drawn, as it is more desirable to have this a little too high than too low. We will now turn our attention to

The Forepart.

Points G, H, and I are already fixed, so we will proceed to apply the front shoulder measure. First deduct the distance from A to B, and sweep, or in other words cast a segment from H by the remainder of front shoulder; now add 1 inch to this for all sizes, but varying it according to the prominence or flatness of the chest; prominent chests are generally found in erect figures, who are frequently very wide across the chest, or, to use another term, have backward shoulders. For this class of figure, add 1½ inches when sweeping from G; whilst of course the reverse applies to stooping figures, who are invariably flat-chested and have forward shoulders, so that we should only add ½ inch for these,

But it must be remembered, that whatever is added on this way, will have to be worked up in the making and pressed back over the prominence of the breast; for it will at once be seen that to add more is to produce a rounder front, and as every figure is hollow down the centre, it does not require aught but a straight line to fit it at that part. This is a vital point in coat cutting, and well repays a little study; but we shall have to leave that for the present. Having fixed the neck point, we turn our attention to the over-shoulder measure, and apply it by first deducting the distance from 9 to W, and sweep by the remainder from H, but putting the finger on the tape at I before sweeping; the reason for this is, that the tape in measuring goes round the scye, so we apply it in like manner. Now measure the width of the back shoulder seam from B to M, and make the front shoulder a trifle, say ¼ inch, narrower, measuring from F, and draw shoulder seam by rounding it a good ½ inch at D. The front of scye may now be formed, and if a guide is desired, a line may be drawn from the end of the shoulder seam to I, and hollow from ⅜ to ½ an inch, carefully noting that it runs well with the back when placed in a closing position at the shoulder. A well shaped scye should have as much of a horseshoe shape as possible, particulary hollow just above J, and well up at the back of sidebody.

Now measure across from F to V ⅙ of the neck measure as previously fixed, and find point V X on a parallel with F, taking the line at H G as a guide; having done this, make it a pivot and sweep the gorge, or, better still, use a pair of compasses to shape the gorge from F to P; then draw a line through P to G from X; the end of the lapel at P should always be *straight*, so that the drawing seam of the collar is straight, a point which adds much to the beauty of

any coat. Now measure across the waist, and allow the same for making, &c., as at the chest, 2 inches; and continue the line from G to L, which finds the actual centre of the front, such as the lapel seam of a Frock or a garment fastening with hooks and eyes. S is made as far below L as R is below the line of waist at J, but this may be varied either higher or lower, and should generally be made to harmonize with the length of the vest, providing it is worn of the average length; as far as the fitting is concerned it makes no difference, as any variation at this part would be adjusted when cutting the skirt, which we will now proceed to deal with.

The Skirt System.

Square down from line R T S to 9 Z 9 inches for all sizes, and come out 1 inch, and draw a line from R through this point; then add on ½ an inch of round as shown on the Diagram; now measure off the length, allowing 1 inch for making up; take out ¼ inch at Q and a trifle at S, so as to make it fit snug at front. It only now remains to add on the button-stand to the forepart, and arrange the run of the front; the amount to add on for button-stand varies according to the style of edge desired: for a bound edge add on 1 inch, for a swelled edge 1¼, and for a double stitched 1½. Now locate the position of the buttons, and arrange them so that there is the same distance between the waist seam and the bottom hole as there is between the other holes. Now comes the one great point of style — the sweep, which shows the touch of the master hand, needing a capacity to produce harmony of outline, combined with your customer's ideal of what he desires, as far as you can imagine. It has been our aim in the draft to produce one of those medium styles which suit the majority, and we leave our readers to judge whether it is

such as they would consider good style. Doubtless many of the junior aspirants for fame in the cutting room will be able to study its outline with advantage, not only in the run of the front but in the general details of all the various parts. We do not think it necessary to give a lengthy description of the back skirts, as the Diagram is explicit enough to guide anyone in that direction; ½ an inch only should be added to the length taken for making up.

The Special Features.

Much of the beauty of the Morning Coat is to be traced to the graceful way in which it follows the outline of the figure, fitting over the prominences and defining the hollows in such a way as to blend the outline of the body in the greatest harmony. Especially is this the case with the back, where the seams are arranged so as to enable provision to be made for the prominence of the blades, and bring the garment in at the waist in accordance with the requirements of the figure; provision being made for the seat and hips by a little judicious manipulation of the skirt. The hang of the pleats is undoubtedly a feature requiring special attention in order to get them to hang fairly without any tendency to gape or overlap; and although it is of course the correct thing to avoid either defect, yet of the two it is better to err on the side of too much rather than too little spring, as nothing looks worse than gaping pleats when the wearer happens to have a few things in his pockets. It should always be the aim of every cutter to get his Morning Coats to set equally well on the figure, whether the coat is buttoned or not. In order to arrive at this desideratum, the balance of the garment must not only be adjusted to a nicety, but the front edge worked up in a proper degree. The skirt, too, should fit as close round the bottom as possible, whilst every provision must be made for the hips. In the case of pockets under flaps being used instead of pleat pockets a little fuller style of skirt is advisable, and the flaps should be cut straighter along the top edge than the skirt, in order to get sufficient spring on the bottom edge, without the necessity of putting on any fulness across the flap; the provision for the hips may then be made in the skirt, either by means of V's or fulness, as the flap going over that part where the fulness is placed would hide the V's, and is an arrangement which not only ensures the fulness being in the right place, but also produces a cleaner fit, as well as securing both skirts being treated alike. As we are giving illustrations and descriptions of most of the varieties of body coats, we will not dwell further on the special features of this important garment, but proceed to give

A Few Hints on Making.

As far as possible this system is arranged to produce a garment requiring the smallest amount of manipulation; yet a little intelligence displayed in this direction will produce results far in advance of one that is merely put together. If tailors generally could be impressed with the fact that they are making garments for human beings, and to know with some degree of accuracy where prominences of breast, blade, and seat were located, and the necessity of providing proper receptacles for them, we should see more garments infused with that form which at once characterizes a well-made coat, and fewer of those flat, lifeless things which would fit a board nearly as well as a living, animate being. To the importance of working up the breast properly, putting the canvas and facing in straighter in the front than the forepart, and providing the receptacle for the breast

in them by puffs taken out at other parts, must be added the importance as well as the necessity of giving more lining wherever the garment fits in a hollow, and less where it goes over a round. If it was pointed out to the workmen that there are certain parts of the body it is considered advisable to build up or tone down, according as the figure was poor or prominent at particular parts, we should get a better class of garment making. But when, as we fear is too often the case in the present day, the workman is ground down to the lowest penny, he has little time to devote to these artistic touches which make all the difference between a ready-made garment and a coat teeming with points of harmony and beauty at every point, such as are occasionally seen on foremen tailors, if nowhere else. It is impossible to point out all these little details which, combined, produce these works of art, so we must content ourselves with just hinting at one or two.

We always advise a little wadding being put round the back scye, as well as the usual amount at the sides, and which should be nicely graded off at both parts. A little shoulder padding put through the shoulders, and just a little wadding in the sleeve heads. Keep the fulness of sleeve head well to the front; commence it 1 inch from the shoulder seam, and keep the sleeves tight round the back scye, put the back easy to the front shoulder, and use the ordinary precautions when putting on the collar, putting it on slightly long in the hollow of gorge, and slightly tight across back neck and in front of neck; shrink the sidebody midway between J and K, and give the sidebody a wee stretch from K to Q; this will allow the garment to go nicely home to the figure at that part, and thereby greatly enhance the fit; keep the skirt fair from R to Q, and spread the fulness for hips over, about 4 inches forward from ½

inch from sideseam at Q, and from T to S keep the skirt tight; put your facing all through the shoulder as from H to T, and see that it is wider than the outside; carry it well below Y of skirt if you possibly can; put a pleat in your lining over the hips, and also leave a little extra width in the back lining; always flash baste your sleeve linings to the seams of sleeve, and finish your cuffs with slits, even though you do not put holes for the buttons. These are a few of the items to be noticed, and if embodied in cutting and making, will be productive of satisfactory results.

D.B. Morning Coats. Dia. 43, Plate 4.

We will now proceed to deal with a garment which has gradually worked it way into popular favour during the past year or two — the D.B. Morning Coat. It is well to have a nice Fashion Plate to show our customers, as that may enable us to arrive at a knowledge of his requirements, as well as induce him to adopt a new style. But having secured this, we have still to produce our pattern before we begin cutting the coat; and that our readers may have everything that can possibly help them in the execution of their daily duties, we give a Diagram of this coat; but after the very full description we gave of the S.B. we will only notice

The Special Features.

Foremost among these must necessarily come the lapel; in fact, in the adjustment of this lies the principal feature to be brought out. It will be found necessary to use the greatest care to get the length of lapel to harmonize with the general get-up of the front, and knowing the general tendency is to get them too short, we caution our readers against cutting them too low in the gorge in the front. Many cutters seem to forget when shaping their lapels, that they represent style only, and have no effect on the fit at all; consequently we always advise the lapel being turned over to see whether the outline harmonizes with the ideal formed when taking the order from the customer. When treating of lapels to our students at the Academy, they invariably appear a bit puzzled at first over the V's; and as probably some of our readers may also be, we will give here the same reply our students generally receive on this matter: If the garment is intended to button pretty well up, it will not be advisable to take out a V; but if, on the other hand, the coat is intended to roll low, a V may be taken out with advantage. The effect of V's are to shorten the length of the outside edge, and as every garment which is intended to button high requires plenty of length at that part, it will at once be seen that it would be wrong to take out a V.

The width of the lapel and general run of the front are both details which are clearly brought out in the Diagram, so that it will be only necessary for us to point out that the line running from X opposite the neck point through to 21½ is the breast line, and where the garment would meet edge to edge. The proper position for the buttons is best found in all D.B. garments by sweeping from any point of the breast line above and below from the eye of the hole; and wherever the sweeps intersect each other locates the button exactly in its right place. It is not intended to illustrate the run of the pattern of the material represented on this Diagram.

D.B. FROCK COAT.
Diagram 44, Plate 5.

The D.B. Frock Coat is undoubtedly the most important garment of the body coat class, and although not so extensively worn as the Morning Coat, it is generally acknowledged the garment above all others that displays the tailor's skill, and pays for high-

class workmanship bestowed on its production. It is also the garment worn on all those important occasions when it is necessary for the wearer to appear full dressed and when the Dress Coat proper would be altogether out of place; in short, it is the Dress Coat for out-of-door wear. Fickle fashion has made great changes in the style in which these are made as compared with a few years ago; and as it is our aim to thoroughly post our readers up in the details of the latest style, we have prepared this Diagram with the view of, as far as possible, illustrating how these are being made at present. Of course there are other varieties, but this appeared to us one of the nicest. The material from which it was made was a very soft, rough make of camel's hair cloth, something like a Vicuna, only much rougher, but still the same dull black. The edges were flat braided; the braid used was a bright make of ribbed satin-faced, stitched on by machine very nicely, forming a splendid contrast to the dull make of the cloth. Then the buttons were of twist, and so matching the braid to a nicety, the silk facings on the lapels being also in harmony. There was just a medium amount of round on the lapel, and little or no light to show between the end of the lapel and collar. The mode of finishing the collar ends is so fully brought out in the Diagram, that any further description would be superfluous, so we will turn our attention to

The Cutting.

As far as the body is concerned, the system is exactly the same as we fully described on page 15, so we will not go over it again, but rather confine our remarks to the special features. Foremost among these is the waist seam which must be so arranged that when the one side overlaps the other they lie exactly on the top of each other,

and so form one continuous run. Then the skirt must be adjusted so that there shall be just enough room for the hips and the action of the leg when walking, and yet be free from any superfluous drapery, to lie in sort of petticoat folds. The quantity, we believe, can be obtained by coming up in the front from the line drawn across at right angles to line 9 O, 2 inches, and then, when finding the run of the front, come up as much *again*, as to * just by 21½; and then get the run of the front by resting one arm of the square on point O, and the corner at *, and drawing the front line at right angles to it. The front is made the same length as the back. It may be useful to say a few words here as regards the fashionable length. This is generally made to just clear the knee. We have been obliged to make our Diagram a trifle short on account of the space, but we should say about 38 full length would be near the correct thing for a figure of 5 feet 9 inches; many, however, are made longer; in fact, some we noticed in the Row, during the end of the last season, were quite 39 or even 40; but most of these very long ones were made from grey worsted, a material much patronized for Frock suits. They were generally made up with silk facings and stitched just on the edge, with either twist or mohair buttons to match.

In cutting the skirt from the cloth about 1 inch is left all down the back, to form the side pleat, and a similar quantity is left as a kind of inlay to be turned in, and form a facing down the front. We will now direct attention to

The Necessary Manipulation.

This could of course be done far easier by a practical demonstration than by a written description, but unfortunately the former method is impossible, so we must make the best of a written description.

We take the skirt before it is seamed to the body part, and before the linen is basted down the pleats, and with a good iron, work the round added opposite 9 well forward till the round is quite gone and a receptacle formed for the hips; but this will not be sufficient, so we take our skirt, and in order to have a guide for the amount to be shrunk away, we take a piece of stay tape and baste the skirt on to it tight, say to the extent of 1 inch, commencing about 5 inches from the back of the skirts. Having done this, we again bring the iron into play and shrink the fulness away, and by this means a much cleaner fitting hip is produced than can be got in any other way, and is especially useful in getting both skirts worked up in the same way, as well as getting the fulness located in the proper position, which should of course be as nearly as possible the position the hip will occupy when the garment is on. In seaming the skirt to the waist, it will not be necessary to full it on at all if this method of manipulation has been followed; though intelligence may here be displayed by carefully avoiding any tendency to stretch the bottom of sidebody, and by keeping it snug (rather tight) at the front. We will not enter into the details of making up the pleat, putting in the pockets, &c., as these are fully understood by every practical cutter; but we would especially call attention to the necessity for a pleat in the lining to provide a receptacle for the hip, as has been produced on the outside.

The Lapel.

The lapel is a very important point in the Frock Coat; indeed, it may almost be said to rule the style, for in its width and outline rest much that is characteristic. The widths of the one we have endeavoured to describe we have marked on the Diagram,

viz., 2 inches at the waist, 3 inches at the widest part, and 2¼ at the top, with a trifle of round put on between these latter parts. In the present Diagram we have cut lapel seam quite straight, and it will also be noticed that it is shorter than the forepart; this, we think, demands a little explanation, In the first place, the lapel must be put on tight opposite the breast, and the fulness well worked over the prominent part of the breast; this could be done to the same extent as was added to the front shoulder when sweeping from 20½. That inch was added, not because the figure required more length to cover the centre of the front; such is opposed to the true state of the case, for there is a decided hollow between the breast or nipples of every man, which clearly indicates that a shortness is required at that part. No, it was rather added to allow of a sufficient receptacle being formed to receive the breast. Now, as we have pointed out before, this 9 inches is only given as a medium quantity to form as it were a basis; but whenever the breasts were prominent, to increase it, and *vice versa*. It is generally acknowledged that erect figures are prominent in the breast, and stooping ones flat, so that the working of this system is in exact accordance with those who insert a wedge in the front for erect figures and take out one for stooping forms; for the more that is added to the front shoulder when sweeping for the neck point from point 20½, the more length is given to the front edge. But whether the figure be erect or stooping, it does not require any difference in the length of the front edge, or, at any rate, not to any appreciable extent; consequently the more that is added, the more the front must be worked up. Herein lies the whole secret of straightness and crookedness, for we are fully convinced that, as originally used, it was never intended to be applied

to the shoulder, but to the *front edge*, which becomes straight or crooked as less or more length is added. Now, every tailor who knows his business puts his lapel seam to the straight of the canvas, and provides the necessary receptacle in this latter by taking out a V under the breast. Many of our very best workmen follow the same course with their facings, a plan which still further enhances the beauty of a well-made coat; for although we always cut our coats to fit with the least degree of manipulation, yet we are not so blind to the excellencies of judicious manipulation, as to say they will produce the highest results with but indifferent workmanship. In the contrary, if we had a set of workmen trained to our ideas, we should introduce many little variations, the principles of which we endeavour to elucidate in these pages.

Thus, it will be seen we cut our lapel with the sewing-to-edge the same as the edge should be, and not as we have cut it, for the purpose of providing breast room. Although this style of lapel suits a garment buttoning up to the height shown, for other styles, such as turning higher or rolling lower, a variation in the length of the outer edge is required; thus, for a garment turning high, the outside edge should be lengthened, which will have the effect of making the sewing-to-edge hollow; the reverse is the case with the rolling low coat. Then the lapel should be turned over on the forepart to see that the waist seam runs the same, and to avoid any angle which might occur. We now think we have touched on the more important points to be observed, many of which, although noticed under the heading of Frock Coats, are equally applicable to other styles, wherever the same principle is involved.

DRESS COATS.
Diagrams 45 and 46. Plate 6.
The Special Features

Of this class of garment are all embodied in diagram 45, which illustrates the roll collar style, that being the one now almost universally patronized by the better classes of society.

To arrange the run or shape of the roll requires very great care, and readily shows the good or bad taste of the operator. There are many ways of arranging the forepart, lapel, and collar, but the one illustrated is the same as is adopted by those cutters who are cutting these garments every day, and they assure us that having tried other methods, they find this to produce the most artistic results. It allows full scope for that variation in outline which a trained eye and good taste would dictate. It will at once be seen that the front is cut away, in the style generally adopted for roll collar vests, the lapel being very short, whilst the collar is necessarily that much longer, and so governs the shape of the roll. As far as the cutting of the body part is concerned, there is really very little variation to the method adopted for the Frock Coat as previously described. The variations introduced are made on account of style, taste, and material. They may be briefly summarised as, first, a lighter, smarter outline to the garment generally. As an illustration of this, we would point out that the back is made a trifle narrower, being only 1¾ wide at natural waist, and cut bare to the width of the back. Second, in the style of front and skirt. The details of the former we have just explained, as far as the roll is concerned, so that the only further point we need call attention to is that the waist is cut to the nett size, *i.e.*, the combined,

widths of back, sidebody, and forepart agrees with the half waist, allowing nothing for seams.

Dealing with the skirt, these are generally cut much longer than any other kind of under coat, a very good guide being to make the entire length of the coat an inch or two less than twice the fashion length of back. In our diagram it will be noticed we have turned back the end of skirt, as the Plate was not long enough to allow of its being drawn to the full length to this ¼ inch scale, which scale we think conveys the general outline of these special garments much better than the smaller one. It will be observed the front of skirt is dropped 1 inch from forepart above A, which is done to counteract any tendency to looseness at B; the width of the strap is generally 1½ inches at A, and the slightest bit wider at C. From A to B of the strap is made one-third of the distance from A to E, whilst from C to D at bottom is made 1 inch less than half A E; the front edge of skirt from C F to B is slightly rounded, and bottom part made to run up in front, which feature is shown in the diagram; and our readers will understand that part of the diagram from F to C and C to D is turned up from the bottom.

Turning our attention to the third point of variation; on account of the material it will be noticed we have only allowed 2 inches over the breast measure, from 9 to 20, instead of 2½ as in most of our draughts; or, if the measure is taken from the back-seam, then 1½ inches over measures. The material from which Dress Coats are invariably made are very thin, much more so than the average cloths used for Frocks, Morning Coats, or Lounges; hence this variation, which is done, not because it is a Dress Coat, but because it is made from a thin material. We should do exactly the same were we cutting the same material in either of the styles mentioned. Thinking many of our readers would be able to understand the features we have introduced in this diagram better, if they saw the variations marked on a Frock Coat body, we have prepared

Diagram 46

Which also shows the ordinary style of lapel. The back is narrowed a ¼ inch as per dotted lines from F to G, care being used at N that the balance remains unaltered; to ensure this it would be as well to draw a horizontal line as shown at N. A ¼ of an inch is taken off the underarm seam from H to I, and the front shoulder is narrowed ¼ inch at H to make it harmonize with the back. The front is cut away at K, so that the combined width of back, sidebody, and forepart measures the *nett* waist measure, from J to K being arranged entirely to taste, as it governs the width of the lapel. As present taste goes, the lapel should be rather light, hence it is customary to cut away ½ or ¾ of an inch from the front of breast for a proportionate figure; but as this is entirely a matter of style, it would be advisable to draw the crease edge line, and then turn the pattern over to see whether it meets your views of what the turn of a Dress Coat should be. The gorge is lowered at J from 1 to 2 inches, and in order to get a straight drawing seam to your collar, the distance from the hollow of gorge to the front at J should be made straight or nearly so. The lowering at this part is done so that the step, or part where the collar end and top of lapels come, should be arranged in harmony with the style of front generally, and although only a trifle, is still a point on which much taste may be displayed, and has a great effect on the finished garment. The lapel for this style of front may be either cut with a straight sewing to edge, or hollowed

½ to ¾ of an inch as described by us in the section on lapels, which our readers should refer to, as the lapel of a Dress Coat is a very important feature, and we described the principles on which they were cut very fully therein.

Considerable difference of opinion exists amongst high-class cutters of the present day as to the correct alterations to be made for a Dress coat from a Frock body. Some say the shoulder should be straightened, others contend it should be crookened; some lengthen the front and others shorten it, and as they all have had considerable experience in this branch, presumably with success, it seems strange that such apparently opposite methods should both produce successful results. But when, as in many other apparent contradictions, the various methods propounded are analyzed, as they recently were at one of our leading societies, it is found, that although working in such different directions, the pattern at the finish produced such a striking resemblance as to astonish the members. This may appear strange to many of our readers, but those of the thinking, investigating class, know how subtle are the laws of cause and effect, and how an alteration made at one part will counterbalance an alteration made at another part and reduce it to a nullity. This is a feature present-day cutters would do well to develop. It will of course require patient investigation, but that, alone will enable us to get at the true principles of cutting. It has been urged that because a Dress Coat is worn unbuttoned, it should be cut with special features on this account; but to this it is replied, that as most Morning Coats, Lounges, &c., of the present day are more generally worn unbuttoned than buttoned, they should be cut to fit in the former way equally well with the Dress Coat, the buttoning being merely lapping the fronts and buttoning it. This we fully

endorse. As an illustration, a Clerical Frock Coat was prepared, tried on, and found to be an excellent fit. It then had the fronts altered as shown in diagram 46, and the skirts cut away, rebasted with lapels on the front, and the result was as good a fitting Dress Coat as it had been previously a Clerical Frock. This, we feel sure, will interest many of our readers who only have these garments to cut very occasionally, and when they do come are rather frightened of them. To such we say: If you can cut a good fitting Morning Coat, you can do ditto for a Dress Coat; the variations in skirt and front are only in style, and we have given as many hints as possible on these points, so there should be no difficulty. We will now conclude these remarks on Dress Coats by giving a few

Hints on Materials, Making, &c.

The materials mostly used are a very fine diagonal, known as a Dress twill, much finer than a corkscrew; a soft wool or vicuna; and, but very occasionally, black superfine, which latter is now fast dying out, and is left for the patronage of livery servants, waiters, &c. The Dress twill is undoubtedly the most popular, and the edges are either left bluff or corded and stitched behind. Silk facings are universally adopted for both styles. *Moiré* or watered silk obtains much favour in the roll collar style. The skirt is generally lined with cloth, the only exception being when it is lined silk, but when faced through with the same material it makes a nice, firm skirt. The pockets are generally put in the pleat, and often made of white, so as not to soil the handkerchief, gloves, &c. An inside breast pocket is either put in one or both sides, which is often kept very forward, low down, and small, so as to make it convenient as a card pocket. The facing of forepart is continued to the bottom of straps in one piece, the skirt facing joining it just behind B. One very important feature in Dress Coats is to get the length of forepart and strap to agree with the length of vest, and should receive carefull attention.

CLERICAL FROCK COAT.
Plate 7. Diagram 47.

Talking the other day to a well known clerical tailor, of the peculiarities of that class of customer, he said: "If you wish to succeed as a clerical tailor, you must be possessed of unlimited patience, for you will frequently have to listen to firstly, secondly, thirdly, and finally on the special features to be infused in the garment for which the order is being taken". There can be no doubt clergymen are amongst the most fastidious customers the tailor has to cater for. Although the special features of the Clerical Frock may seem so plain that they do not admit of much variety, yet the height of the collar, the opening in front, the angle at which the collar recedes at front, are just a few of the items of variation; and when we add, that the gentleman above referred to showed us a pattern book of over 80 different patterns of stand collars, it will be seen that indeed there is some hair-splitting differences to be provided for; so that it must not be inferred the clerical. tailor has an easy time of it. Oh no! He has quite as many troubles as the ordinary tailor, and perhaps just a few more. There is very little scope left for the tailor's individual taste, for, apart altogether from fit, there are details which must be carried out with the utmost accuracy. The details vary of course for different classes, so that the tailor has to find out not only whether his customer is rich or poor, but also whether he is High Church or Low Church,

whether he is an ordinary clerical or a dignitary, as there are distinctive differences in their dress. There is one point that must not be lost sight of in dealing with all garments of this class, viz., that a S.B. Frock Coat with stand collar has a tendency to make the wearer appear narrow-chested, so that care must be exercised to avoid this as much as possible.

The Peculiarities of Clergymen.

As regards their figure, first there is a tendency to corpulency — we believe it will be found that quite four-fifths of them are inclined to be corpulent. This may arise from sedentary habits, or it may be the contented mind they possess, which is a continual feast. Be that as it may, the fact remains the same. The next peculiarity we have noticed is a slight stoop, a kind of head forward, which must not be overlooked; whilst there is the third feature, which, though it has been told to the trade again and again, is nevertheless a point not to be overlooked, viz., the use of their arms when preaching. We believe one celebrated orator undertook to make as much impression on his audience with his hands visible and his face hid, as a rival did with his face in view but his hands hid. Whether he succeeded or not we cannot say, but doubtless many clergymen use their hands very much, with wonderfully good effect, too. The moral of this for the tailor is, to use special care to prevent the scye being too deep, as the effect of a too deep scye when the arms are lifted is anything but comfortable or artistic, so that in all clerical coats a too deep scye is to be avoided.

In Cutting,

All these features have to be noticed, and we have endeavoured to embody them in diagram 47, which also shows the usual

amount of opening at I, generally about 2 or 2½ inches, but may be varied according to taste; clergymen as a rule, however, like to adhere to the regular style, being of a somewhat conservative turn of mind. In order to get the buttons exactly down the centre of front, it will be necessary to allow only about ¾ of an inch on the button-hole side, and 1½ inches on the button side, when the eye of the hole will come exactly on the breast line of the one forepart, and the buttons on the breast line of the other. This is especially important at the top, so that the button may come exactly in the centre of the opening. The skirts are made long and fairly close fitting. In the diagram we have been obliged to make the skirt short, on account of the size of the diagram plate, but our readers can easily extend to any length. As will be noticed, we have come down from E to C 2 inches, by which to get the angle to square A 9, the run of front being found by coming down from A to B also 2 inches, and squaring from E B to H. The length is extended to measure, making A G and E H equal.

The Special Feature

Of the Clerical Frock is its plainness. The collar of the coat must harmonize with the customer's ideas in relation to the linen collar he is wearing, and it will be necessary when trying the coat on, to get the customer to put on the usual collar he wears, as it is essential that the white linen should show an equal quantity all the way round. These coats are seldom worn buttoned more than one at the top, and should really be made to keep their place on the figure when worn unbuttoned. To meet this, some tailors cut an advanced (or what some would call a straight) neck point; but we see no special reason for any exception to be made in this way; true, care must be

taken to get the neck the right size, but this can be done without interfering with the usual location of the neck point. Further, there is the same prominence of the chest to be provided for, and even more, provision being necessary for the pockets in the breast, of which there are often two. In introducing this garment we hinted at

Variations in Details

For the different ranks, if we may so term the various stations in the church. The principal difference between a Frock Coat for a dignitary and an ordinary clergyman, is in the buttons. The ordinary number up the front is six, but a dean or bishop usually has seven. The arrangement of buttons on the cuff is also different. The dignitary usually has three buttons placed across the cuff, as is usual with some naval garments. But apart from any variation for rank, there is the deviations for personal taste. Take, for instance, the matter of collars: not only are there the variety of stand collars we have previously noticed, but there are turn-down collars, such as the Prussian and Panteen, which find a certain number of supporters. Then, again, is the matter of length: some, especially the High Church party, like them long; others, comparatively short; and though the general length would be about the bend of the knee, yet this may be varied to taste of wearer.

Materials mostly used.

Superfine broad cloth was the material exclusively used for these garments, till a few years ago some of the enterprising firms of Clerical tailors introduced their Clerical serge, which had the great advantage of being cheap and wearing well. At the present time Vicunas, Serges, Diagonals, and Superfines are all used. The latter

material is naturally preferred by the more elderly clergy, whilst the three former, and especially black Serges and Vicunas that are not too rough, are preferred by the younger men. The general style of edge for the Superfine is bluff, and for the Serges, Vicunas, and Worsteds, a single-stitched edge; such ornamentation as binding or fancy buttons being altogether out of place on garments of this class, everything being kept as plain as possible.

CLERICAL DRESS COAT.
Diagram 48. Plate 8.

It is only when the cutter takes an order for one of the special garments — of military, naval, or clerical dress, that he begins to realize the scope there is in the tailoring trade. For if he is to be a real master of his business, he must thoroughly understand them all. But there are probably few men, indeed, who have a really complete knowledge of the business from beginning to end, and have the details and special features of any and every garment at their fingers' ends. As in every other profession, there are specialists in the tailoring trade, who make it their study to understand the specialities of the class of customers, and the kinds of garments they cater for. London with its vast population and its easy communication with all parts of the world, favours this, and consequently specialists flourish. But with the country towns it is different, and the provincial foreman who is called upon suddenly to make such a garment as forms the subject we are now treating of, is at once brought face to face with a difficulty. It is then he turns to works such as this and realizes, when he finds one containing all the information he desires, what a great boon the trade literature is.

The Clerical Dress Coat

For evening wear is cut as per diagram 48, the details of which may be briefly enumerated. Single-breasted, with the front curve or the run of front similar to a Livery Full Dress Coat, which garment it resembles throughout, but with a difference at the collar. The collar is of the stand type, but does not run in a line with the front, but is kept back to form a step. The fronts are finished in different ways; for the ordinary clergyman there are plain holes and flexible buttons; but for the bishop there are notched holes up the front as on diagram, but we will deal more fully with these presently. Many clergymen wear the ordinary Dress Coat for evening wear, but the garment which is looked upon as the Clerical Dress Coat proper, is as illustrated on diagram. The vest and trousers worn are usually the same as for morning wear, though occasionally the vest is treated in a similar manner to the coat, and cut away at the top to show the shirt in the notched step style, similar to what is worn by smart dressing gentlemen for ordinary wear.

The Bishop's Evening Dress

Has several points of distinction. The coat has six notched holes across the front; these are now usually formed with narrow Russia braid, the art of making a notched hole being now almost, if not quite, obsolete. The braid looks quite as nice, so that we do not think this is a matter of very great regret. Buttons or "deadheads" are placed at the ends of these holes. The length of the top hole should be 5 inches, and the bottom one on the waist seam 2½ inches. Pointed flaps are put on the waist seam, with a button under each point; but the pockets are placed in the pleat, the flaps being merely a matter of style. Gauntlet cuffs with three holes on them is the usual mode of sleeve. The remaining features of bishops' dress are corded: silk Cassock vest, black doeskin breeches, silk stockings, silver buckles on shoes, and to crown all, the beaver "shovel" hat. The material used for these coats is black superfine, and as it is generally acknowledged, that the material allows the fullest scope for the workman to display his skill, we will give a few

Hints on Making.

It is imperative that the strictest attention be paid to the working up of the fronts, collar and step; as the secret of much of the success to be achieved with these garments lies in the careful manipulation of these points, upon which clergyman are notoriously exacting. There is a great art in getting the fronts to go over the breast nicely, and lie snug down the fronts, and as there is no ornamental silk facings, &c. it will be at once apparent that special care must be used to get it to lie snug. The edges are, as usual with all clerical garments, left bluff, and the body, skirt, and collar are lined with black silk. Some cutters put hair cloth through the shoulders and fronts to keep them firm; but on this there is a difference of opinion, many specialists in the clerical line objecting to it, on the ground that it makes them stiff and unyielding, and as such, unsuitable to a clergyman's requirements. The details we have enumerated must be carefully observed at all points; as we hinted in the previous page, clergymen are very particular to adhere to the orthodox style, by which their garments are distinguished. As we pointed out many of the special features of clerical attire in the previous section, our readers cannot do better than turn to it for information on any point that has not been embodied in these remarks. Should any of

our readers take an order for this garment, and not feel competent to cut it, they can obtain a special pattern cut to the measures, and description they may forward, by enclosing 1s. 1d., in stamps, to the *Tailor and Cutter* Office, 93 & 94 Drury Lane, and if they specially order it so, it can be forwarded in a plain envelope. It may be interesting to some of our readers to know that a Barrister's Dress Coat is got up in a very similar way to this, the notch at the collar being omitted, but the fronts are arranged as for the bishop, with notched holes, &c., as previously described.

COACHMAN'S LIVERY FROCK.
Diagrams 49 & 50. Plate 9.

We now come to the more important livery garments, such as the Coachman's Frock, the Footman's Coatee, Livery Overcoats, &c., all of which are special garments every cutter ought to be thoroughly conversant with, not only in their outline, but also in every detail. Before, however, we proceed to deal with the special features of either garment, it will be as well for us to make a few remarks on

The General Features of Liveries.

Plainness should always be one of their leading characteristics; any attempt to follow the present fashion must be carefully avoided. The edges, when not piped with a different colour cloth are invariably finished bluff; that is, without any stitching on the edge. Some fell the edges, others seam and press them open; the latter course, to our mind, is the best, being decidedly the neater. The linings should all be of the plainest possible character, and whenever wadding or padding is required, it should be flash basted in only. For sleeve and vest linings stripes should

be avoided, using silesia or sateen of a self colour. Whilst the cutter should never attempt to follow the present style, yet he must produce a smart and neat fit, as livery servants are usually very particular about their appearance; and as they generally have a considerable amount of influence with their employers, it will always be advisable to do our outmost to meet their whims and fancies, otherwise they will probably do their best to get their garments made elsewhere.

Rules for Selection of Colours.

Having looked at the general features of these garments, we will now give the rules for the selection of the colours of the cloth, buttons, &c., which are usually adopted by livery trades; and although it may not often fall to the tailor to suggest what colour the livery shall be made from, inasmuch as families invariably have their own colours and style, yet it is just as well he should know which is considered the correct thing. Occasionally customers will call who are just starting a livery servant, or they may be dissatisfied with their present colours, on which occasion they look for guidance from the tailor. The body of the coat is generally made from cloth the same colour as the body of the carriage is painted; and in the event of its being edged, the edging should be the same colour as the fine lines, or picking out on the carriage. The buttons are made the same colour as the harness, that is, if the harness fittings are silver plated, the buttons are the same, and if gilt the buttons are gilt. The great coat is generally made from drab Devon, but in the event of that colour not being chosen, it should be made to agree with the colour of the cloth lining of the carriage. These rules are frequently broken unawares, as families have fresh carriages without giving that particular attention to the colour of fittings, which makes all the difference in the effect of a good turn-out or otherwise; and although the exact details of the colours we have mentioned may be deviated from, yet the principle involved in them should be rigidly adhered to, so that harmony may prevail between the colour of the Livery and fittings of the carriage and harness.

These remarks of course apply to all kinds of Livery garments.

COACHMAN'S FROCK COAT.
Diagram 49.

It will at once be seen this style of coat is a single-breasted Frock Coat, to button six holes, cut rather close-fitting at chest, and easy at the waist, a full skirt, a rather forward scye with a forward hanging sleeve, the back cut a trifle wider than for a gent's Frock; flaps across the waist about 9 inches wide, and 3½ to 3¾ deep with pockets under, a ticket pocket in the seam, and generally an inside breast pocket. The flaps are cut to follow the outline of skirt, as in the diagram; the cuff is formed either by a row of stitching, or by putting on a cuff 2 inches deep, with one hole and button above and one below. (See diagram 50.) A long side edge is placed down the back skirt, with three buttons on each, *i.e.*, one at hips, one at bottom, and one a trifle nearer the top than half way between the top and bottom, say ½ an inch nearer; this middle button is sometimes omitted. When they are edged with a different coloured cloth, the edging is put round the collar, down the fronts, up the back skirt, round the flaps and cuffs. The length of skirt is made to come within an inch of the knee; the coat is made to fasten fairly high up, the height of the turn being so arranged that a narrow piping of the vest roll is seen above the coat; the bottom hole is placed in the waist seam. Many coats are now made with the buttons only at the pleats, the actual side edge being omitted.

It will be seen the skirt is rather full, it being advisable to err on the side of too much drapery rather than too little. We have previously pointed out that the more line S is dropped below waist seam the more fulness will be the result, the run of the front being got by letting the square rest on a point as far below hip button as comes down in front, so that run of skirt is squared by A*.

Grooms' Frocks

In their general outline very much resemble those worn by the Coachman, although quite distinct from him, being generally a smaller and smarter man, who likes close and natty-fitting garments. The coat is of the Frock form and, like the Coachman's, is finished with six holes and buttons up the front; as a general rule but sometimes, when the groom is very small in stature, there are only 5 buttons placed up the front, the skirts, however, are shorter, and with grooms who ride, very much shorter, barely coming over the seat. There are several points of difference in the details, foremost amongst which is the absence of flaps and pockets at the hips, these being placed at the pleats. At one time they were always put in the outside pleat, with middle button on the side edge, fastening with a hole, and so securing the mouth of the pocket; but we believe this is now becoming a thing of the past, and that they are more generally put inside the pleats. The side edge, too, is shorter, and frequently pointed; they are usually made about 9 inches long from the hip button. The sleeves are finished in the manner illustrated by diagram 50. These

coats should be made fairly close-fitting, as Grooms will not have anything of a loose or slouchy nature, and when they ride and wear a belt, it is advisable to cut waist smaller still, only allowing 1 inch for making up, otherwise it will form in folds above and below. The edges are finished the same as the Coachman's — bluff, and in the event of their being edged with a different coloured cloth, it is put round the collar, down the fronts, up the backs and round the cuffs. A ticket pocket is generally inserted in the waist seam on the right side, and an inside breast pocket on the left. It is made to fasten well up in the front, and special attention should be given in producing a neat collar and turn, as grooms are very particular on these points of detail. The remark we have made on the sleeves apply to the groom as well, it being advisable to give them a forward-hanging sleeve. The lining in the skirts of these coats is sometimes the same colour as the breeches, *i.e.*, white or drab.

FOOTMAN'S COATEE.
Diagram 51. Plate 10.

A glance at this diagram will show the great difference existing in the outline and details between the Coachman's Frock and the Footman's Coatee, indeed they may hardly be said to have any features in common, for the one garment is intended exclusively for outdoor wear, and the other more especially for indoor service; though of course the Footman has to take his place on the box and receive his lord or lady's orders. The only details in which these are exactly the same as the Coachman's are, 1st, the cuff, as illustrated on diagram 50; and 2nd, the side edge, which latter features can be seen on the diagrams. In general outline, the Coatee resembles a gent's Dress coat, although it is cut much

heavier in style, and the skirts shorter, the general rule as regards length being, that they shall be 2 inches above the knee. They are cut rather larger than the gent's Dress coat, as they are intended to be worn fastened with links at front. With this end in view, they are cut 1 inch over the waist measure; they were at one time made large enough to button at the waist, but the march of the time has left its mark even on liveries. The old style, with snipped collar ends, and buttoning across the front Coatees, are merely relics of the past. Now, links made of two livery buttons fastened together with a split ring or a shank made of thread, is the only style of fastening they have, the size of the waist being arranged as we have described, which allows the garment to be kept easily in position without any drag.

The lapel is cut heavy, as compared with a gent's Dress coat, and has 5 holes, 2 above and 3 below the turn; this arrangement is sometimes reversed, and 3 put above and 2 below; still the former is the livery regulation. The lapel should be cut so that the outside is on the crease, which can easily be done by folding a piece of paper and laying the lapel down with the front along the crease, when the shape at the top can easily be arranged by taking out a rather large V extending down to just below the second hole, as illustrated on diagram 34. This V must of course be arranged so that it comes about ½ an inch back from the edge, so that when it is stoated up a good double edge is the result, which wears much better than the raw edge sometimes used, and which, if the material is not very good soon wears rough and ragged. The sewing to edge of the lapel may be cut quite straight, and it should always be remembered the upper part of the forepart, as shown above the crease line, is arranged quite in accordance with taste, and has no-

thing to do with fit. The gorge must, of course be lowered, say 1 or 1½ inches, and the front part kept straight, in order to get a straight drawing seam to the collar, which always produces a much better effect than a curved one. Care must be used so that the back scye is not hollowed out too inuch, which also applies to the underside sleeve, in order that no drag may be felt when waiting at table. These coats are specially liable to split across the front of scye, just above point 16½; and for this reason the front and over-shoulder measures may be lengthened a quarter of an inch or so, though that would of course, not facilitate the fit at the waist behind, but give rather more room in the shoulders.

The Skirt

Is cut on the same lines as a Dress Coat skirt, but the waist being larger and shorter in the length, it has a different appearance. The length of the strap is one-third of the width from hip button to lapel seam; and the width 1½ at front to 1¾ where it joins the tail; the width of the bottom of the tail is made 1 inch less than half the distance from hip button to lapel seam; the sword flap is put in as nearly as possible in the centre of the skirt, about 11 inches long by 2 wide, and pointed as shown; this is really only a piece of cloth sewn on the same as the skirt; it is sewn on down the straight side towards the front and then turned over, and either stitched round or the edges piped to match the edge. Many firms put the sword-flap with the top to run with the waist seam, but we think better harmony prevails when it is put on in the position shown in diagram. The skirt is always faced through with the same cloth, and all the remarks we have made about the plainness of the trimming applies with equal force to the coatee.

The sleeve should be made rather forward hanging, as for the coachman. All the buttons are plugged, with the exception of the cuff buttons; that being the rule with all livery buttons used for ornament only. When a coatee is edged with a piping of different colour cloth, it is put up the fronts, round the collar, along the bottom of skirt strap, down front of skirt but not along the bottom, up the opening of back skirts, on the top button and pointed side of sword flap and round the cuffs.

Page's Jacket. Diagram 52.

With the view of dealing with all the every-day Livery Garments, we have given a small diagram of Page's Jacket, and from which our readers will readily be able to follow the outline. The back is cut on the crease, left pointed at bottom, and running shapely up over the hips, the fronts buttoning to throat, and fastened with ball buttons put rather thick together, the usual number being 14 or 16 according to the size of boy. These garments should be very smart fitting, a little wadding being generally resorted to in order to improve the figure as much as possible; this may be stitched in, it being the exception to the ordinary run of livery garments in this particular. Many varieties are introduced, such as studs put up each front, &c., but the style illustrated on diagram is the most usual.

FULL DRESS LIVERY COATS.

The garments worn by Livery Servants for full dress are often of the most elaborate nature, cloth or velvet being used generally for the body, and which is most elaborately trimmed with embroidery and tracing braid. As far as the cutting is concerned, the style of cut very much resembles the Clerical Dress Coats, diagram 48, with the exception that there is no notch left at the end of the collar, it being brought to the end of the front. The fronts are cut away from the breast (where they fasten with two hooks and eyes) above and below, the Coachman's being much less cut away than the Footman's. The cuffs are generally of the gauntlet style, and these too are trimmed in harmony with the fronts. The skirts are lined to match the breeches which latter are often made of plush.

The Vest is made no collar style, fastening with hook and eyes down the front, made to open low. The length is much longer than usual, and the pockets are often covered with flaps. The vest is trimmed in harmony with the coat, though it is often made from different material.

We will not deal further with these very exceptional garments here, but proceed to treat of

LIVERY OVERCOATS.
Diagram 53. Plate 11.

Probably there is no special class of garment the average cutter will be more likely to meet than Livery Overcoats, for there are few trades of any pretensions to respectability that do not come in for their share of these.

In dealing with the special feature of Liveries, it will always be the best plan for the cutter to follow the garments the servant is then wearing, for the conservatism of families is often prominently brought out in such details. For instance, some have the seams of their overcoats slated and double-stitched, others have them plain, and the cutter would be overlooking a serious item indeed, if he omitted a feature of such importance.

Diagram 53. Plate 11.

It is not our intention to go over the system again point by point, as we feel sure all our readers know it by the time they

have reached this point in the work, but as there are several variations we will briefly point them out. The usual additions of ⅜ inch have been made to the across chest, front, and over shoulder, and natural waist measure, and the back increased ¼ inch as for other overcoats, and 3½ allowed beyond the chest and waist taken over the vest, whilst for those who prefer taking the measure over the coat, 2½ will be ample. In the course of our experience we have found a great tendency for fulness in the back section of these coats, and the reason attributed by us as its cause, is, the material being thick and stubborn, would not bend itself to the hollows of the waist, and consequently we take out less between back and sidebody as at 3½, 4½; we also reduced the usual 1 inch at back at 17½ to ½ an inch. Knowing also the difficulty in working up the breast, we only add ¾ to the front shoulder, but making the front shoulder a trifle longer, as 13, for what in the ordinary way would have been 12⅞. The lapel is cut by the forepart, making it about 2½ inches wide, top and bottom, the top being run off as shown so that the top button may be arranged for the collar to be slipped under it, a great advantage with collars of this class which are often very unruly.

The special features

Of this coat apply generally to all kinds of servants. The back is cut 3 inches wide at the waist; a 12 inch side edge placed at the back of the skirts (see diagram). The skirts are cut very full (which are produced by dropping line A 3½ by which to square down to 9 and then coming up to 3½ to find* see lapel diagram resting the square on it and the top bottom of skirt at back, by which to find the run of front). The Prussian Collar and the 6 buttons up the front, are the same for all classes, but in the arrangement of the pockets comes a distinguishing feature. The diagram illustrates a Coachman's Coat whose pockets are placed in the waist, and the length of skirt reaches to the middle of top boots; the Footman and the Groom both have their pockets in the pleats. The former has his skirts very long, reaching almost to the ankle; whilst the Groom's coat only reaches to a little below the knees. A great variation exists in the manner of putting in the ticket pocket; some put them in as illustrated, others put them in with an ordinary flap, and others again put them in the waist seam.

A few Hints on Making

Will probably be useful. All the buttons except those on the right forepart are plugged, being for ornament only, and in order to get the collar to fit nicely, and appear level all the way round, the left gorge must be lowered a seam in front. The edges of the lapel, collar, flaps and side edges are left raw and double-stitched as shown, the skirt generally has an inlay down the front which forms a facing when turned in. The body is lined with tweed and the skirts with shalloon; the fall of the collar is often left unlined except on the edge, this of course for the sake of thinness, the same principle is applied to the pocket flaps, &c. The cutter should always make it a point of taking the skirts out of the cloth without wheel pieces, as apart from the extra work it gives, it certainly does not improve the appearance. All that is necessary to fold the skirt pattern over and lay it on the crease edge. A very good lay of this will be found in the Prize Essay on Cutting by Model Patterns (published at this office), and as it does not require an inch more material, the cutter should never overlook this. The usual quantity required for an overcoat is from 2⅝ to 2⅞, say an average of 2¾.

MILITARY GARMENTS.

We have now come to another series of special garments which the cutter is liable to be called upon to execute at any time, and as they have many distinctive features, the diagrams will doubtless be of service.

In military garments, the attention to details of regulation is everything, and as there are so many varieties, to remember the details of all appears almost impossible, and as it is quite unnecessary, we should not advise our readers to start with that end in view. Every facility is offered by the War Office in this respect, they not only publish a book containing all the dress regulations of the army, at the nominal price of one shilling and sixpence, but they also keep sealed patterns of every garment at the War Office for inspection by the trade, so that if the details of any garment is desired, all that the cutter has to do is to call at the War Office in Pall Mall, and ask to be shown the particular garment he desires, and every facility will be afforded them. We believe they are even allowed to take a tracing of the braiding on the cuffs which is done by placing a sheet of thin paper on the top of the design desired, and whilst keeping it firm to rub over it with a piece of shoemaker's heel-ball, when the distinct outline of the tracing will appear in the same way as the school boys often produce on their school books by rubbing the paper covers with a piece of soft pencil.

In this work we have selected the three most general styles of body garments, viz,, the Tunic, the Mess Jackets, and the Doublet, leaving the Patrol Jacket, &c., for a future work on three seamers, &c.

The Special Features

Of military garments are as follows: They are cut wide at the back neck, and with a short shoulder slope, the aim being to bring the shoulder seam well on to the shoulder. All backs are cut on the crease, and the hind arm of sleeve generally runs with the sideseam, which sometimes necessitates a modification of the run of the sideseam. A small (narrow) sidebody is generally considered good taste, but care must be exercised not to overdo this, as is often done in garments for general wear. The waist seam is arranged to come 1 inch below the natural waist, and a belt hook is placed on the hips for those who wear belts.

Plenty of room is left in cutting, at the chest, as this part is generally padded up a bit, but the waist is cut to 1 inch over the waist measure, it being very important that the waist should fit tight, especially when a belt is worn. The little padding that is placed on the front should be kept well *above* the chest, there is never any wadding put in the back, except for de_formed figures, which are practically never met with to any serious extent in the army. First class trades line their garments with Silk Serge and Quilt it ½ inch diamonds, this of course applies to officer's garments; those for privates have the wadding flash basted in only, the colour of the lining is a matter of regimental taste, the unwritten rule being to follow the colour of the facings or the prevailing regimental colour.

The skirts of tunics should be made as close-fitting as possible, ½ an inch of fulness is generally sufficient to put on over the hips.

It will be noticed there is only a small amount left on beyond the breast line on the hole side, and extra button stand being left on the button side, this is done to get the eye of the hole and the buttons to come exact on the centre. Some trades cut the button side only to come to the breast line, and then sew on a button stand, but the more general plan in the best trades is to

cut the extra button stand on the front. We will now proceed to deal with each garment; and take first

THE MILITARY TUNIC.
Diagram 54.

The special features we have just mentioned have all been introduced in this diagram; the back neck is made an inch wider, and consequently V I is rather less than usual; 2½ inch has been allowed for making up, to allow for a little wadding. An extra ¼ inch has been taken out between back and sidebody and sidebody and forepart, to allow of the waist going close home to the figure, as it must do when kept on by the belt, and only 1 inch allowed over the waist measure. The collar is rounded at the top in front; and the height must not exceed 2 inches. The regulation depth of skirt for officers 5 feet 9 inches is as follows: — Field Marshals, General Officers and Colonels on the Staff, Artillery, Engineers, Foot Guards, Infantry Regiments, Army Service Corps and Departments generally — 10 inches. For General Staff, Cavalry and Rifle Regiments — 9 inches. The variation for different heights is ⅛ inch for each inch of difference in the height.

If the tunic is braided, the braid, or ornaments are placed at equal distances apart, unless specially stated otherwise in the *"Dress Regulation of the Army"*.

Buttons are generally an inch in diameter, small buttons ¾ inch. When loops of lace or cord are worn across the breast, the top loops reach to the sleeve seams, and those at the waist are made 4 inches long. It is impossible for us to give all the official instructions for every kind of tunic, so we merely give a specimen, which will give our readers some idea of the minute detail contained in the *"Dress Regulation of the Army"*.

Field Marshal.

Tunic — Scarlet cloth, with blue cloth collar and cuffs. The collar embroidered in gold. The cuffs round, 3 inches deep, with gold embroidery 2¼ inches deep round the top; a scarlet flap on each sleeve, 6½ inches deep and 2¼ wide, embroidered in gold. A similar flap on each skirt behind, ½ inch shorter than the length of the skirt and 2½ inches wide; 8 buttons down the front, 3 on each flap; 2 at the waist behind. The front, collar, cuffs, and flaps edged with white cloth, 3⁄16 inch wide. An aiguillette of gold wire cord, ¼ inch in diameter, with gilt embossed tags will be worn. The aiguillette is attached to a plaited strap on the right shoulder, of round gold cord 3⁄16 inch in diameter, intertwined with a small dead gold cord. A similar strap on the left shoulder. On each strap, crossed batons of crimson velvet and gold, on a wreath of laurel embroidered in silver, with a crown in silver above, a small gilt button at the top.

The Military Frock Coat.

We have not given a diagram of this, as it is cut on just the same lines as an ordinary Frock, the regulation length of the skirt is 17 inches for a figure of 5 feet 9 inches. The official regulations are very explicit, so we take the following extract from the instructions for the clothing of the General Staff: —

Frock — Blue cloth, double-breasted. Rolling-collar; the front and collar edged with ¾ inch black mohair braid. An Austrian knot of black Russia braid on each sleeve, reaching to 6 inches from the bottom of the cuff; 5 loops of black Russia braid on each side of the breast, fastening with black olivets; 2 olivets at the waist behind. The skirts lined with black. Shoulder-straps of the same material as the

garment, edged with ½ inch black mohair braid, except at the base; black netted button at the top. Badges of rank in gold. mmIn addition to this there is the

Single Breasted Frock

as worn by the Cavalry for undress. The following description will be as concise as anything we can put: —

Frock — Blue cloth, single-breasted. Stand-up collar, ornamented with figured braiding; and figured braiding on each sleeve, extending to 12 inches from the bottom of the cuff. 6 loops of ¾ inch black braid down the front on each side, with 2 olivets on each loop, the top loops reaching to the shoulder seams, those at the waist 4 inches long; ¾ inch braid on the outer seams of sleeves and back seams, with eyes and fringe at the waist, and tassels on the back-skirts. Hooks and eyes in front. The skirt lined with black silk. Shoulder straps of the same material as the garment, edged with ½ inch black mohair braid, except at the base; black netted button at the top. Badges of rank in gold.

For the special adaptations to the various departments, we must refer our readers to the Official Hand Book which will be forwarded from our office post free for 1s. 9d.

Mess Jacket. Diagram 55. Plate 13.

We do not think our readers will need a very lengthy description of the manner of cutting this, as they will be able to gather the method of applying the measures by referring to the diagram. As with all other military garments, there is a great variety of trimming and finishing in matter of detail, so we content ourselves by giving the regulations for Staff-Generals:

Mess-Jacket — Scarlet cloth, edged all round, including the collar, with 1 inch

oak-leaf lace forming barrel at the bottom of the back seams. Blue cloth collar and cuffs, the collar in front, with a loop of gold braid at the bottom to fasten across the neck. A tracing of ⅜ inch gold chain gimp along the bottom of the collar. A row of gilt studs in front on the left side. The cuffs pointed and edged with 1 inch oak-leaf lace, the lace extending to 6¼ inches from the bottom of the cuff. Shoulder-straps of blue cloth, edged with ⅜ inch oak-leaf lace, except at the base. A small gilt button at the top. Badges of rank as for tunic, except that they are smaller, and that the hilt of the sword is in gold. Scarlet silk lining.

The Stable or Shell Jacket is cut in the same manner as the above, the special details for each division will be found in the book referred to. We now come to

The Highland Doublet. Dia. 56. Plate 14.

As will be seen, this is cut on precisely the same lines as the tunic, as far as the body part is concerned; the variation of skirts being its special features, and as the outlines of these are very clearly brought out in Plate 14, we will once more lay before our readers the official regulations as laid down for Highland Regiments.

(ROYAL HIGHLANDERS, SEAFRONT HIGHLANDERS, CAMERON HIGHLANDERS, ARGYLL AND SUTHERLAND HIGHLANDERS.)

Doublet. — Scarlet cloth, with collar and cuffs of the regimental facings. The collar laced and braided according to rank, as for Infantry of the Line. Gauntlet cuffs, 4 inches deep in front and 6 inches at the back, edged with ⅝ inch lace round the top and down the back seam, 3 loops of gold braid, with buttons on each cuff. 8 buttons in front, and 2 at the waist behind. Inverness skirts, 6½ inches deep, with skirt-flaps 6 inches deep; 3 loops of gold braid

with buttons on each skirt-flap. The front collar, skirts and flaps edged with white cloth, ¼ inch wide, and the skirts and flaps lined with white. Shoulder straps of twisted round gold cord, universal pattern, lined with scarlet; a small button of regimental pattern at the top. Badges of rank in silver.

Field Officers have a second bar of lace round the top of the cuff, and ½ inch lace round the skirts and skirt-flaps. Colonels have 2 lines of braid, and Lieutenant-Colonels, 1 line within the lace on the cuffs. mmCaptains have a line of braid within the lace on the cuffs.

Lieutenants have the same lace on the cuffs as Captains, but without the line of braid.

The second bars of lace and lines of braid on the cuffs are to be ¼ inch apart.

The skirts or tashes vary in length; and as most of our readers will gather from the diagrams, they are double, that is — there is a smaller one on the top of the other. The dotted line on the front tash is intended to convey the position of the pocket usually placed in the under tash in front. The left back skirt, as will be noticed, is smaller than the other, which is done with the object of letting them appear both the same size when the left one is overlapping the right. The tashes do not meet in front, being kept from 1½ to 2 inches from the edge of the forepart.

Having now dealt with all kinds of Military Body Garments, we will pass on to treat of another special class: —

NAVAL GARMENTS. Plates 15 & 16.

We now come to another special branch upon which there are clear and concise instructions laid down by those in authority; but inasmuch as the Navy embraces a very much wider area than Military, and as there are a great many other regulations upon

which it is necessary to be well posted up, the book in which these particulars are to be found is published every quarter, and is called *The Navy List*, the price of same is 3s. Anyone who has orders for Naval Garments, and are not thoroughly conversant with their every detail, will find it a positive necessity. As with the Military Garments, there are sealed patterns kept for the inspection of the trade, the places being the Admiralty, Whitehall; so that all metropolitan tailors have to do, is to pay the Admiralty a visit, and take notes of the details of the garment they may desire.

The Navy is divided into two branches, viz., a Military branch and a Civil branch; the former wear double-breasted coats, with the exception of the Midshipman and Cadet, and the latter S.B. garments. The body coats that are worn embrace a Full Dress Coat, diagram 57, which is always worn buttoned and the collar hooked. The Frock Coat as far as the cutting is concerned, is like 44; the variations on point of finish we will notice presently. This is worn buttoned 4 buttons. There is the Undress Tail Coat as illustrated by the left hand figure on the bottom of Plate 15, and which is cut the same as diagram 57, with the necessary variation of lapel and collar for turning; this also is worn buttoned 4. In addition to these there is the Undress Coat, which is cut like a Frock Coat, but without skirts. The following are official regulations as taken from the last Navy List: —

THE FULL DRESS COAT.
Figure 2.

For all Commissioned Officers, except Chief Gunners, Chief Boatswains, and Chief Carpenters, — Blue Cloth, double-breasted, 8 buttons in each row, 3 inches apart across the chest, the skirt to begin at one-fifth the circumferance from the front edge, and lined with white kerseymere; one button at the bottom of each plait, and two in the waist seam behind. Pointed blue flaps on skirt and three buttons under them.

For Flag Officers and Commodores, 1st Class — Flaps on skirt laced all round with 1¾ inch lace. A row of 1 inch lace to encircle the hip buttons and form a point above them on the seam.

For Commodores, 2nd Class, and Captains — Flaps on skirt laced all round with 1½ inch lace. A row of 1 inch lace to encircle the hip buttons and form a point above them on the seam.

For Commanders — Flaps on skirt, laced all round with 1½ inch lace

For Lieutenants and Sub-Lieutenants — Flaps on skirt laced all round with 1 inch lace.

For Chief Gunners, Chief Boatswains, and Chief Carpenters and Warrant Officers — Blue cloth, double-breasted, 8 buttons in each row, to button the four lower buttons, fall-down collar, round cuffs with three buttons, and notched holes of blue twist thereon; pointed flaps with notched holes of blue twist and buttons under them to correspond; 3 buttons in the fold of the plait of the skirt; the skirt to begin at one-fifth the circumference from the front edge.

Collar of the Full Dress Coat.

For all Commissioned Officers, except Chief Gunners, Chief Boatswains, and Chief Carpenters — White cloth, the front edges slightly sloped, and fitted with a black silk tongue to cover the space between them; fastened at the bottom with one hook and eye.

To be trimmed with gold lace according to rank, namely: —
Flag Officers — 1½ inch top and front edges, ⅝ inch lower edge.
Captains and Commanders — 1¼ inch top and front edges, ½ inch lower edge.
Lieutenants and Sub-Lieutenants —
1 inch top and front edges,
½ inch lower edge.

Not less ⅛ inch of white to show between the upper and the lower lace. If necessary, the lower lace may be partly on the coat.

Cuffs of the Full Dress Coat.

For all Commissioned Officers, except Chief Gunners, Chief Boatswains, and Chief Carpenters — Blue cuffs, with a white pointed sash with 3 buttons, and rows of distinction lace according to rank; the dimensions of the sash are: 7 inches high at the points, 6½ inches at the seam, and 2⅜ inches wide at the centre. The outside edge of the slash bound with gold lace according to rank, namely: — Flag Officers and Commodore, 1st Class, 1 inch wide; Commodore, 2nd Class, Captains and Commanders, ¾ inch wide; Lieutenants and Sub-Lieutenants ½ inch wide.

Rows of distinction lace: — For Flag Officers and Commodore, Ist Class — A band of 1¾ inch lace round the cuffs, with rows of ⅝ of an inch distinction lace round the sleeve above the cuff, according to rank, viz: — Admiral of the Fleet 4 rows; Admiral of the Fleet, 3 rows; Vice-Admiral, 2 rows; Rear-Admiral and Commodore, 1st Class, 1 row. The upper row to form a circle 2 inches in diameter, in the centre of the upper sleeve.

For Commodore, 2nd Class — A band of 1¾ inch lace round the cuffs, and a circle of 1¾ inch in diameter, formed of half-inch distinction lace above it.

For Captains, rows; Commanders, 3 rows of ½ inch lace. Lieutenants over 8 years' seniority, 2 rows of ½ inch lace with a row of ¼ inch lace between them.

Lieutenants under 8 years' seniority, 2 rows; Sub-Lieutenant, 1 row; Chief Gunners and Chief Boatswains, 1 row of ½ inch lace.

Gunners and Boatswains over 10 years' seniority 1 row of a ¼ inch lace. The upper row to form a circle 1¾ inch in diameter

in the middle of the sleeve.

For Officers of the Civil Branch — The cuffs will have the same number of rows as those of Officers of the corresponding ranks in the Military Branch, but the upper row will be straight instead of being formed into a circle, and the space between the rows will be of coloured cloth according to branch.

Assistant Paymasters of 6 years' seniority; Engineers under 6 years' seniority, 1 row of ¼ inch lace above 1 row of ½ inch lace. The space between each row of distinction lace to be one ¼ of an inch.

Frock Coat.

For all Officers, except Midshipmen, Naval Cadets, Assistant Clerks — Blue cloth, double-breasted, with padded turn-down collar; cut for 6 buttons, but to have 5 buttons on each breast, to button 4 buttons; the width of lapel to be 3 inches at fourth button, tapering to 2¼ inches at waist seam; 2 buttons on the hips, with side edges in plait of skirt extending half-way down the skirt, with a button at bottom of each side edge; for Officers 5 feet 9 inches in height, length of coat 38 inches, with a proportionate variation for difference in height. Lining, black silk, Hook for sword belt. Round cuffs, sleeves laced as in full dress. Omitting the slash. Shoulders fitted for epaulettes; the fittings covered with blue cloth.

Undress Tail Coat.

For all Commissioned Officers (excert Chief Gunners, Chief Boatswains, and Chief Carpenters), Midshipmen over 18 years of age, and Clerks — Blue cloth, double-breasted, 6 button holes in each row, 4 in the turn and 2 below, padded turn-down collar; pointed flaps with 3 notched holes of black twist and buttons under; 1 button at the bottom of each plait, and 2 in the waist seam behind. Round cuffs, the sleeves laced,

as in full dress, omitting the slash. Shoulders fitted for epaulettes.

Undress Coat.

For all Officers — Blue cloth, with padded turn-down collar: the length to be sufficient to cover the hips; double-breasted, with 5 holes and buttons at equal distance on each side, to button 4. Pockets, without flaps, at the sides, in a line with the lower button, and 1 outside left breast pocket. An opening 5 inches long at the bottom of each side seam. Round cuffs, the sleeves laced as in full dress, omitting the slash.

Midshipman's Full Dress and Undress Coat.
Diagram 58 & 59.

Blue cloth, single-breasted, with 9 notched holes on each breast, and 3 on each cuff and pocket flap, with buttons to correspond, lined with white statd up collar, with white turn back on each side of the collar, with notched hole and button.

Midshipman's Jacket. Diagram 69.

Blue cloth, single-breasted, with 7 buttons; 3 notched holes of black twist on each cuff with buttons to correspond; a stand-up collar with a hook and eye, and with a white turnback and button-hole of white twist 1⅔ inches long, with a corresponding button. When worn it is always to be hooked at the top.

The material from which these uniforms are made is smooth blue cloth, the substance varying according to the climate. Silk facings are prohibited.

The occasions on which the various garments are worn, may all be seen clearly described in the Navy List.

On Plate 16, we give illustrations of the various gold lace used for trimming the cuffs and edges, and as each specifies for which officer it is used, it is unnecessary for us to do so again here.

Diagram 58 illustrates the style in which Full and Undress Tail Coats are cut for the Civil branch; the variations of trimming, &c., being in accordance with the rank they hold, and which will be found clearly detailed in the Navy List.

The dress of Chaplains in the ordinary Clericals is as shown on Plates 7 and 8, the regulations stating: —

On board his Ship, and on all occasions when the Officers of the Ship are ordered to appear in uniform, a Chaplain shall wear a clerical collar or stock, or a collar and white tie, and shall be dressed in other respects in such a manner as shall clearly indicate his profession.

On all occasions when Officers are required to appear in Frock Coats, the Chaplain's dress shall be a black cloth frock coat and waistcoat, and trousers which are either black or of a dark mixture.

A Chaplain's ordinary mess dress shall be a Clerical Court Coat, a waistcoat and trousers, all of black cloth; but, in the evening when Officers wear full dress, or ball dress, the waistcoat shall be a black silk cassock one, and, instead of trousers, shall be worn black cloth knee breeches, with black silk stockings and patent leather shoes, with silver or plated buckles.

WORKING MEN'S COATS.
Diagram 70. Plate 17.

From Bond Street to Whitechapel is not more than three miles, yet in that short distance what a difference exists in the manner of living of those who frequent each neighbourhood. Equally varied also is the style and cut of their clothes. In the former locality the lord, duke, or earl lounges or dines at his club in the latest style of evening dress, whilst in the other

you may see the "ikey lads" in their "pearlies and bell bottoms", swaggering along the streets as proud of their "kick-sies" as the lord could be of his faultless dress suit, or immaculate shirt front, with its diamond stud flashing with all the brilliancy of first water. We have devoted so many of these pages to garments suitable for the prince, that we feel sure that those of our readers who only cater for that class will not complain if we devote this one to the requirements of the working man.

The Special Features

Of whose garments are fully brought out in the diagram of Coster's coat on Plate 17, and may be equally applied to all styles of garments for the working man. This class have large shoulders; the blades are rather prominent; the chest is comparatively narrow, and the waist perhaps scarcely so delicate as the masher who wears corsets. These features demand a special style of cut; the scye deeper, larger, and more forward; the back wider; and the waist not being so hollow, we have only come in ½ inch at 17; the blades being more prominent, we have taken out an extra ¼ inch between back and sidebody. The depth of scye and front shoulder measures are both larger than normal, whilst the over shoulder measure is increased in greater ratio still, so allowing for the development of muscles at the top of the arm. Then the great feature of the garment being ease, an extra ½ inch is allowed for making up, so making the front of scye fully ¾ inch further from centre of back seam than the ordinary morning coat.

The Skirt

Too, needs considerably more fulness or drapery to allow sufficient room for the capacious pockets they so much patronize, whilst the flaps are of the most ornamental

design, velvet being frequently used for these, with buttons placed in all directions; indeed they seem to glory in the number of buttons they can put on their garments. The method adopted to give the desired amount of fulness to the skirt is the same in principle as illustrated on the Frock coat skirt, viz., instead of squaring down to 9 by a line drawn level with bottom of side-body and forepart, lower it two inches (see dot and dash line) in front, and then square it at right angles to this line. Care must be used only to add ¾ inch above this line, as at point ¾, just below the under arm seam, or the fit will be destroyed, landing the extra spring intended to come over the side at the back, and so making the pleats overlap.

The Sleeve

Should be arranged with a decided forward hanging tendency. This may be adjusted in the working of the system, if a block pattern is being used, by inserting a wedge in the hind arm, opposite the top of the forearm, say of ¾ inch; which will allow of the arms being brought forward without any strain across the back, though it will, of course, land a little superfluous material at the top of the hind arm, when the arm rests at the side. The underside should not be too much hollowed out; as, if the scye is cut at all extra deep, and the under sleeve hollowed, the whole weight of the coat will rest on the muscles directly the arm is raised, and produce anything but that effect of ease we have been aiming at. Doubtless our readers will be able to gather the features to be noticed from these remarks.

Hints on Making.

In making and trimming garments of this class, the use to which the garments will be put should always be considered, and as hard wear will always be associated with these, the trimmings should be strong, and the work genuine and honest. The utmost attention should be given to the pocket stays, and generally the aim should be to produce a garment suited for hard wear. On the other hand, clumsiness should be carefully avoided; for it will often be found that the working man will be quite as keen a critic as many of the higher classes. Many working men can appreciate skilled workmanship, and their eye is frequently as trained, owing to their particular calling, as any artist's.

These remarks, so far, of course, apply to all classes; we will now point out the peculiar features the coster patronizes. He invariably has his sleeves long, his cuffs made to button, and faced with velvet, which he turns back, making a finish to the sleeve in consonance with the neck, with its velvet Prussian collar. The seams are almost invariably raised, and the flaps and side edges are sometimes made of velvet, though perhaps the more frequent way is to finish the breast and ticket pockets with velvet corners. Certainly the style they adopt is entirely their own, and embodies many of the principles of artistic tailoring, and which when seen, applied to the higher class trades and especially the ladies, we are ready to admire; and yet, when seen in the coster's coat we are apt to call low and vulgar. But the tailor who caters for this class can fully appreciate it, all forming, as it does, part of the essential features of his ideal garment. And after all, it matters not in what class of trade we are engaged, or from what class of society we find our customers, the same principle must guide us. To get in touch with our customers, we have their ideal of a perfect garment fixed in our mind, and then with a fair knowledge of cause and effect in tailoring, we can execute it with credit to ourselves, pleasure to our customers, and profit to our employers. These are the principles which underlie all true success; and if we embody them in our business, it will matter not whether our customers are peers or peasants, costers or princes, they will all alike be satisfied with our efforts, and so lay the foundation for a prosperous career.

We will not dwell further on this garment, as a study of the diagram will supply all the necessary details, as well as illustrate the principles of cutting in their practical application; thus putting our readers in possession of a few ideas on how to infuse ease in a garment, and give ample room in the scye section.

POLICE TUNIC.
Diagram 71. Plate 18.

This garment is really nothing more than a S.B. Frock made to button up to the neck, the usual number of buttons is 8. Special care should be used to get the neck to fit close, so that no ruffian may be able to get his hand inside the collar in a scuffle; this is a point we have frequently had attention called to in our own experience with garments of this class; a black leather stock is placed inside the collar in front. Policemen being generally very large in the front shoulder, and not unfrequently of erect type, plenty of room should be given them in the shoulders and sleeves, as a good deal depends on the free use of their arms. The skirt is cut rather full, and generally about 12 inches deep, 1 button is put in the pleat behind as illustrated on the diagram. The only other special feature we think it is necessary to notice, is, that being worn with the belt, only 1 inch is allowed over the waist. In all other points the diagram is very explicit, and as these garments vary so much in different parts of the country, and as they are in-

variably made up to the usual pattern, it is quite unnecessary for us to describe it more in detail, suffice it to say diagram 71 illustrates the usual style for the metropolitan police. The cloth is usually a dark blue, the body and skirt lined with twill or Italian, the buttons of special patterns from white metal. The edges are either bluff or stitched on the edge, and the cuff is generally plain. Figures and letters are placed on the collar, and these require a little care to get them to run true and be straight; they are of white metal, and can be obtained from any wholesale trimming house. The Sergeant's chevron is generally formed from Silver Russia Braid; 3 rows with a point in the centre pointing downwards, the rows being about 1 inch to 1¼ inch apart. The position of this is about midway between elbow and shoulder, and should of course be kept well on the top of the arm.

ETON JACKET AND VEST.
Diagrams 72 to 75. Plate 19.

Probably there is no garment the high-class tailor is called upon to make for the juvenile community more frequently than the Eton jacket; for, however much ready-made garments may find favour with the parents, the Eton jacket almost invariably falls to the tailor; consequently there are few respectable trades but are frequently called upon to make this garment. It takes the same place in juvenile attire that the Frock and Dress coats do for gentlemen. It is worn on all occasions demanding either full or semi-dress. As usually worn, it is made to come about 3 or 4 inches below the natural waist, and finished at the back with a point (see diagram 72), indeed, this point is looked upon as one of its special features; and yet, strange as it may seem, it is seldom seen at Eton, where this garment forms the every-day apparel of the

rising generation, attending the various colleges or public schools with which Eton and the surrounding neighbourhood abounds. It is also generally supposed that the Eton boys wear the white linen collar outside the jacket, and the Harrow boys inside, but whether any regulation exists on this particular we do not know, but we believe such to be the custom. This is a point upon which it will be well to enquire at the time of taking the order; for although the Eton fashion finds favour in most cases, yet we have had the unpleasant experiences of having to make alterations on this account; for it will be easily understood, that if the collar is to be worn inside the jacket, the neck will require enlarging; however, as we wish to draw a diagram to suit the majority, we have adapted it to the style most generally worn.

Diagram 72.

It will at once be seen, there are very few variations from the working of the system, as fully explained in the section treating on Morning coats, such alterations being more on account of the style than anything else; such for instance in the back, which is cut on the crease, and only 1¼ wide at waist. It will be observed we have taken out the ordinary 1½ between the back and sidebody, but this should always be adjusted in accordance with the developments of the figure at that part. We should be overlooking one of the most important features to be observed when cutting for juveniles, if we did not call attention to the general tendency of all juveniles to erectness with a corresponding flatness of the back; indeed the juvenile often favours the corpulent build, and requires almost identical treatment. These features have been embodied to a certain extent in the diagram, as well as in the scale on page 15. We will not enter fully

into the developments of growth in juveniles, or trace the various relations one part of the body bears to another at the various ages, such for instance as is found in the anatomical fact that the head at birth is nearly one-fourth of the total height of the body, and gradually develops, till at the age of 16 it bears the relation of 1 to 7½. All this our readers will find fully treated in Part I. of "The Cutter's Practical Guide", and from which they will be readily able to gather what we have so often pointed out, that at different ages the shape of the body varies, one part developing rapidly and another slowly; hence it is necessary we should give them varied treatment. In order to make this as simple as possible for our readers, we have arranged a sectional scale (see page 15), compiled from the result of our own practice, and combining most of the special features to be found in the various sizes and ages. At the same time, it should be borne in mind, we always advocate the sectional measures being taken on every customer direct, and which, if taken with care and intelligence, define the special features to be observed when cutting the garment.

The Special Features.

Care should be taken to give plenty of spring over the hips at the side — a point this which frequently gives considerable trouble, especially if the inlay, which is generally left along that part, is not properly worked up. The length of the front should be made to just cover the vest in a similar way to the gent's Dress coat, and although a little extra length is permisable, yet few things look worse than a jacket 4 or 5 inches below the vest, giving the impression of "wearing out my brothers old coat".

Care should also be taken not to get the

lapel too heavy, or the step too high. The diagram illustrates a neat medium style, and is produced by lowering the gorge 1 inch, and then growing a lapel to the breast line of 1¾ at top, 2¼ at the widest part, and only ¾ inch at the bottom. 3 buttons are put up the front, but the jacket is never worn buttoned; a flower hole is sometimes put in the turn, but it is as often left plain. A good facing should be put through the forepart, in which one and often two in breast pockets are inserted. The back should be shrunk at point 14, and we have sometimes found it advisable to put a half ply of wadding all over the top of the back.

At present these jackets are invariably made from a fine black diagonal, a kind of dress twill or corkscrew, with the edges bound as diagram. The binding is never carried round the bottom, which is generally left bluff, the inlay being merely turned up all along that part. This material has entirely superceded the old superfine black cloth, being so much more useful and less liable to tear in every day wear. There seems, however, a tendency to adopt the cheviots and vicunas, which have been so popular, but these are not general.

The style of sleeve generally worn is illustrated on diagram 73, which is the ordinary hole and button cuff, with the braid put on cuff, as indicated, and brought to the end of the slit.

The Vest. Diagrams 74 & 75.

This is generally of the no collar type, and is of course finished in the same way, and made from the same material as the jacket. This style is often varied, the roll being adopted for dress or semi-dress occasions, such as parties or balls; still, for general purposes the style shown on the

diagram is the one most generally adopted. Before concluding this subject, it may be well for us to make a few remarks on the trousers as generally worn, and so complete the suit.

The Trousers

Are invariably made from black, same as jacket and vest, for dress or semi-dress wear; but for school wear they are frequently made from any dark neat material, such as West of England Hairline; it should, however, be remembered that the correct thing is black, and any variation from that must be particularly neat, only being permissable on account of its increased usefulness and wear resisting qualities for school use. One point to be specially remembered is, that the seat of these trousers shows very conspicuously, so that it is not allowable to put in seat pieces or take out cuts that will show below the jacket, as such would give a "short of material" impression. Care should also be taken in cutting these to avoid all surplus material (only allowing 1½ over seat instead of 2 inches), and to get them to fit as clean as possible at the back of thighs, just under the ball of the seat; and, with this end in view, it will be as well to cut the seat seam a little more hollow than usual at the fork, and also to have the hams shrunk so as to get as clean a fit as possible. It is just such little details as these that are noticed by parents, and add materially to the success and renown of the tailor. The pockets of the trousers are preferably put in across the top, as the side style gape so much; but this is one of those points wherein it will be necessary to consult the wishes of your customer, it not being of very great importance which plan is adopted, though the cross, being much neater, is decidedly preferable.

MORNING COAT FOR CORPULENT FIGURE.
Diagram 76. Plate 20.

The garment we have selected for our present illustration is one that doubless every cutter has to tackle occasionally; and as the corpulent figure has several important deviations from the normal, it cannot fail to be useful to the bulk of our readers. The corpulent figure is often found in customers who have passed the prime of life, say between 45 and 60, when there seems to be a very general tendency to develop fat. Whatever may be the causes which produce corpulency we may not stay to inquire, we know that there are corpulent figures, and our study will be, how to clothe them successfully.

The Special Features

Of this class of figure are: Squareness of shoulder or shortness of neck, shortness of body, erectness of position, and the large development in the front. There are also minor features, such as straightness of back, flatness of blades, poorness of hips, and shortness of arm. A study of the development of human growth shows us the skeleton or framework of the corpulent body is the same as when it was, say 30 or 40 breast, and as all this development in circumference has taken place without any increase in the height, the body at once looses its proportion. It is in figures such as these that direct measurement must always show to advantage, and prove its superiority over any divisional or graduating method. Take as an example the height of neck, it is positively less than in the normal 36. The framework of bones is the same, the development of flesh giving all the increase; and although we readily and fully acknowledge the fact that the shoulder bones always remain near the surface of the skin (see figure 2, point 1, the Cutter's Practical Guide, Part I), still there is a slight addition of fat, which reduces the height of neck, whilst the increased width of shoulder intensifies this; so that instead of the irregular triangle having lines, 3 inches, and 7 at right angles, for two of its sides, it has then 2¾ by 9, which will at once convey to our readers the alteration in the shape of the shoulder, as represented by the third side. But apart from this, let us consider

How the corpulency is distributed.

We find there is a very small increase in the back, but there is perceptible filling up of the hollow below the blades, and at the sides there are rolls of fat; but even the combined development of back and sides represents little more than one-third of the disproportion, the remainder going to the front, necessitating the man to alter his carriage and stand more erect, in order to retain his equilibrium, at the same time giving the arms a decided backward hanging tendency. We have previously explained how to decide the amount of corpulency or disproportion, but as some of our readers may have forgotten this, we will refresh their memory. Our normal pattern is arranged to fit a man four inches smaller in the waist than chest. This then is our ideal, so that when we find a man 48 chest and 50 waist, we say a man 48 chest ought to be 44 waist, but he is 50; the difference between what he is and what he ought to be is 6 inches; and this constitutes the amount of disproportion which forms the basis of our calculations.

The practical application then of all this is, that as the back is flat we only come in ½ inch at natural waist to draw back seam; as the blades are less prominent, we take out less between back and sidebody, and in order to locate the ⅙ of the disproportion at the side and increase the length of front in due ratio to cover the prominence, we come in from A to * ⅙ of the disproportion, in this case 1 inch. Line A is drawn at right angles to depth of scye line; one-fourth of the breast from the back seam; and instead of continuing this depth of scye line straight across, it is drawn at right angles to 12¼ and *, across the forepart, which really swings the forepart round, adding on ⅙ of the disproportion at the side, and at the same time providing the extra length so necessary. It also allows the pattern being drawn without any part overlapping another, thus allowing better opportunities for the infusion of style.

It will be noticed that a V is taken out between forepart and skirt in the front, and in order to explain the reason of this, we shall touch upon a very important principle, viz., that down the *centre* of every figure there is a decided hollow, the human figure being symmetrical, or, in other words, the right side being the exact copy of the left, in reverse, shows us that the development does not take place exactly at the centre of front, and culminate in a point, but locates itself on either side; and we find that a garment cut with a straight breast line, as from V to 29¾, will suit this figure just as well as the thin or proportionate one, if the surplus size produced by that method is taken away by means of V's — see dotted lines at Q. Those, however, who object to the use of V's, produce the same effect by rounding their breast line and waist seam.

Hints on Making.

It is certainly the correct method to draw, in and work back any round there is on the forepart, as at 29¾, locating the fulness over the prominence of the stomach. The same process being repeated at Q, makes it, fit snug below. We think a V taken out

improves the style, for it introduces a vertical line and so apparently reduces the width of such division; but whether it is drawn in, or a V is taken out, the effect will be the same on the waist seam, viz., to straighten it.

We have already referred to the flatness of the hips; this should be remembered when sewing on the skirt, the same amount of fulness and manipulation not being needed as for the smart young gent with small waist and prominent hips.

The sleeves must not be given a too forward hang, as the figure being erect, a rather backward hang will be found more suitable.

The collar should be kept fairly low in the stand, as the shortness of neck in figures of this class makes them very sensitive to anything like a high collar, 1 inch being often quite sufficient stand to give them.

General Remarks.

Some of our readers may imagine when they look at the diagram that the scye is very close. This appearance is brought about by the pattern being wedged round, and it will be necessary to put the finger on 12¼ and let the front wedge round to the amount of the disproportion, in order to arrive at a proper idea of the real shape of the scye. The style of Morning coat we have selected — the button 1 or 3 — is the style and character big men are supposed to look best in; the fronts being cut away at waist, and the skirts cut well forward, reduces the extreme prominence, and brings them nearer the outline of the proportionate figure.

And now a word or two about the material. Never dress a big man in a conspicuous pattern, or a very light colour, and on no account dress him in garments made from cloth, the prominent feature of which is a large check, for that would intensify his width without adding to his his height. Stripes, on the other hand, give height and reduce the width; but even these must be used with great care and caution, for one great aim in dealing with a corpulent man must be to avoid making him conspicuous. So that a neat bird's-eye pattern, a plain grey twill, or a black would be the most suitable. Black apparently reduces the size of the wearer, absorbing all the light that falls on it; whereas those shades, such as white, red, yellow, &c., which reflect the light, make the figure appear much larger, a feature certainly not desirable in a man 48 chest, 50 waist, which is the size we have selected for our illustration, taking the sectional measures from the scale on page 15.

Frock Coat for Corpulent Figure.
Diagram 77. Plate 21.

In order to illustrate the same workings as we have just described, for corpulency to the Frock Coat, we have prepared this diagram; but as all we have remarked of the corpulent Morning Coat applies also to this, it is not necessary we should again repeat. The lapel is cut in the ordinary way, and so also is the skirt; with the latter it may be as well to use every precaution to prevent fulness below the pit of the stomach, and with that end in view it should be put on tight at the wavy mark of forepart. There must not be an excessive amount of fulness in the sleeve head, or this would make the figure appear squarer than he is already, which is not desirable. The collar should be treated as for the erect figure, and generally the treatment should have the aim of apparently reducing the size of the figure rather than otherwise.

In looking over the foregoing pages to see what has been omitted, or what could be added to make it of more practical use to the cutter, we thought it would be as well to give concise rules for finding the four quantities, viz., depth of scye, front shoulder, across chest, and over shoulder, by divisions of the breast. They are as follows: Depth of scye equals one-fourth breast; front shoulder equals one-third plus ½ an inch; across chest equals 1 inch less than one-fourth breast; over shoulder 1 inch less than half; taking these divisions of a size or two smaller in the large sizes and of a size or two larger than the actual breast measure indicates for the small siześ. But there is another way which, though less reliable than the direct measurement method, is nevertheless a distinct advance on the breast measure, viz., the application of the shoulder measure.

The Shoulder Measure

Is taken from the backseam some 5 or 6 inches from the neck (a trifle higher or lower will not make any appreciable difference). The measure is taken from this point over the shoulder and back to the same point again. In the average figure this measure will agree with three-fourths of the breast measure, but as people's shoulders vary irrespective of the size of their chest, this proportion will often vary. The method of applying it is to take two-thirds of this measure to form a working scale, and then making the depth of scye one-half, the front shoulder two-thirds plus ½ an inch, the over shoulder 1 inch less than scale, and the front of scye will be best found by this method by measuring from the centre of back to front of scye two-thirds of the scale. To those who fancy they are unable to take direct measures accurately this will doubtless be of service, as it is a distinct advance on the breast measure system.

There are doubtless many

Unusual Garments

Of the Body Coat class we have not yet touched upon, but we have little doubt our readers will find diagrams of similar ones in these pages, and so by the aid of a little judgment will be able to draft them; for instance, the gents' Newmarket is cut very similar to the Livery Overcoat, with variations of detail to smarten it up a bit. Then, again, there is the old-fashioned Paletot, which seems to be rapidly making its way to public favour. This is cut on the same principle as a Frock Coat, with the skirt, forepart, and lapel grown together, the underarm seam being occasionally taken a little way into the skirt, to provide the necessary fulness for the hips. The Postillion Jacket is cut on the same lines as the Highland Doublet, but of course minus the tashes. It is generally finished with a belt at the bottom, and is often fastened with hooks and eyes up the front with a row of studs up the edge, although the more general way is to fasten it up the front with holes and buttons. There are many other garments of an exceptional character which we have not touched upon, but they may be successfully treated in the same way as those we have mentioned, the principal feature of them being embodied in some one or other of the various diagrams we have given.

CONCLUSION.

We now come to the closing paragraph, and if we have succeeded in gathering from the pages of experience a few hints which may be of use to others following the same pathway, we shall not have laboured in vain. We know the profession is fully competent to form a true estimate of the value of this work and so we refrain of our own judgment from any expression, as praise might be looked upon as egotism and depreciation as mock humility; so we send the second part of "The Cutter's Practical Guide" forth on its own merits, with the sincere desire that it may be, as its title indicates, a *Practical* Guide to all desirous of more light on the treatment of the many garments they have to deal with in their daily experience.

THE AUTHOR.

Plates of Diagrams

ILLUSTRATING

 THIS WORK.

Plate 1.

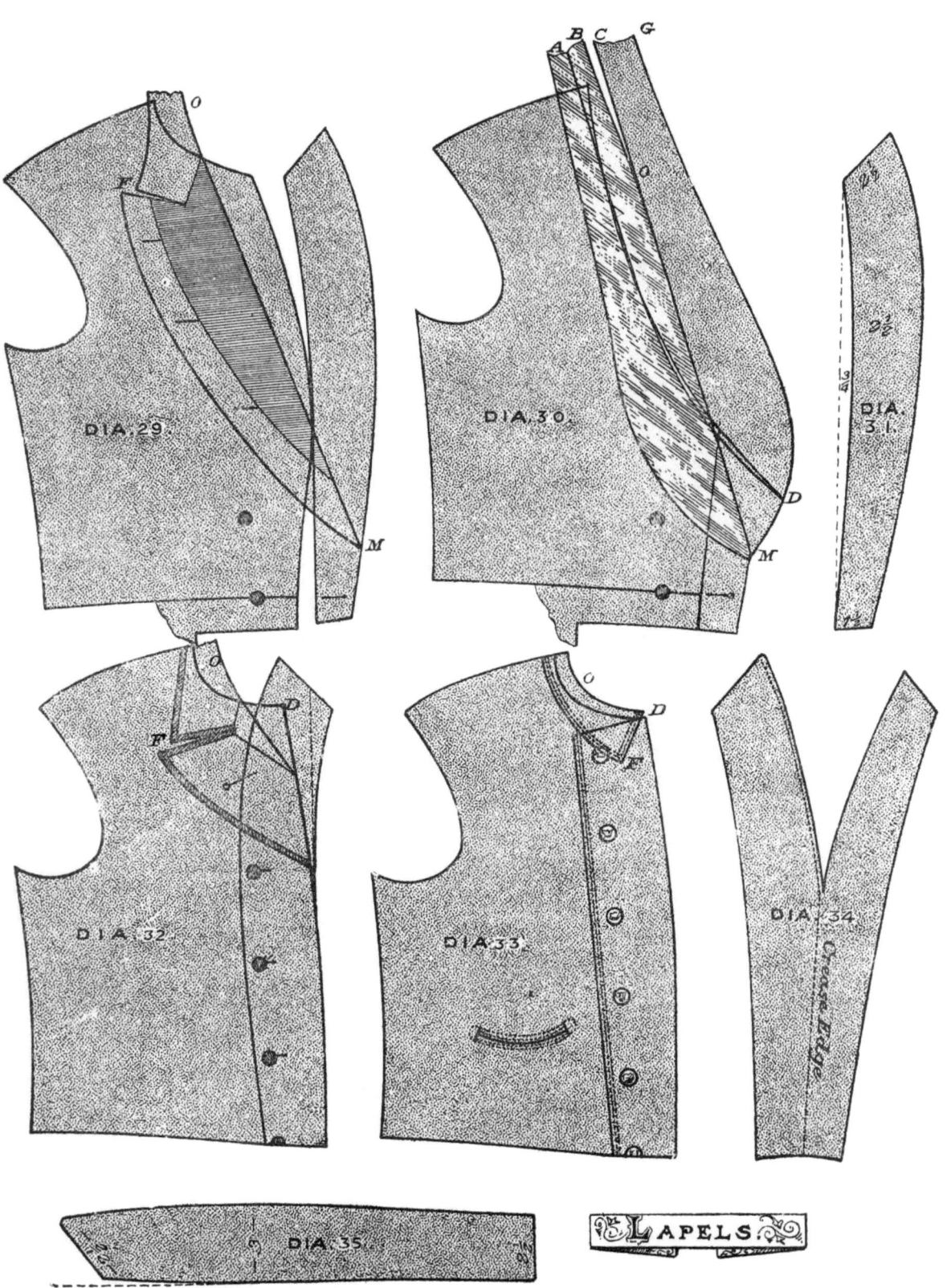

Plate 2.

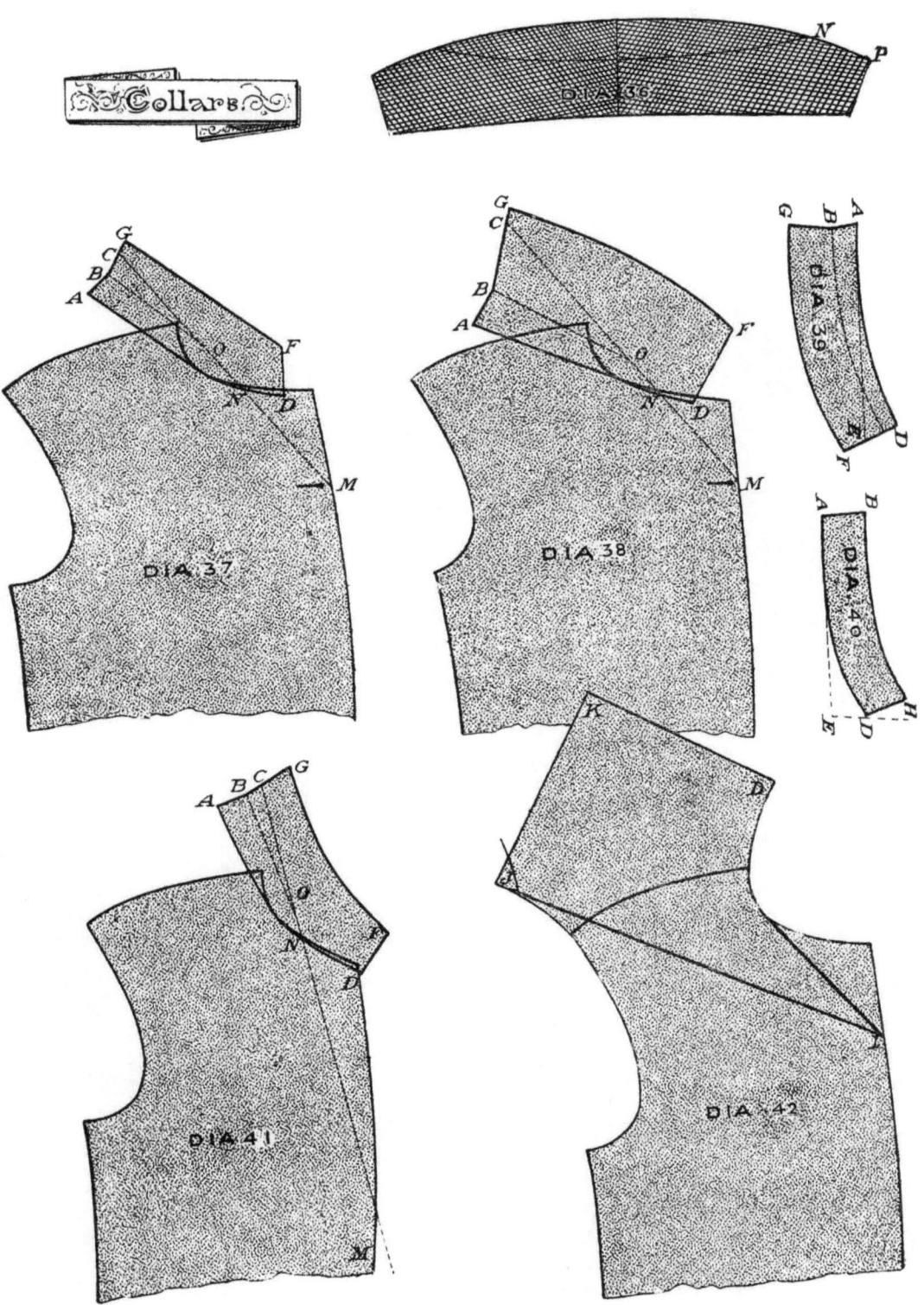

Plate 3.

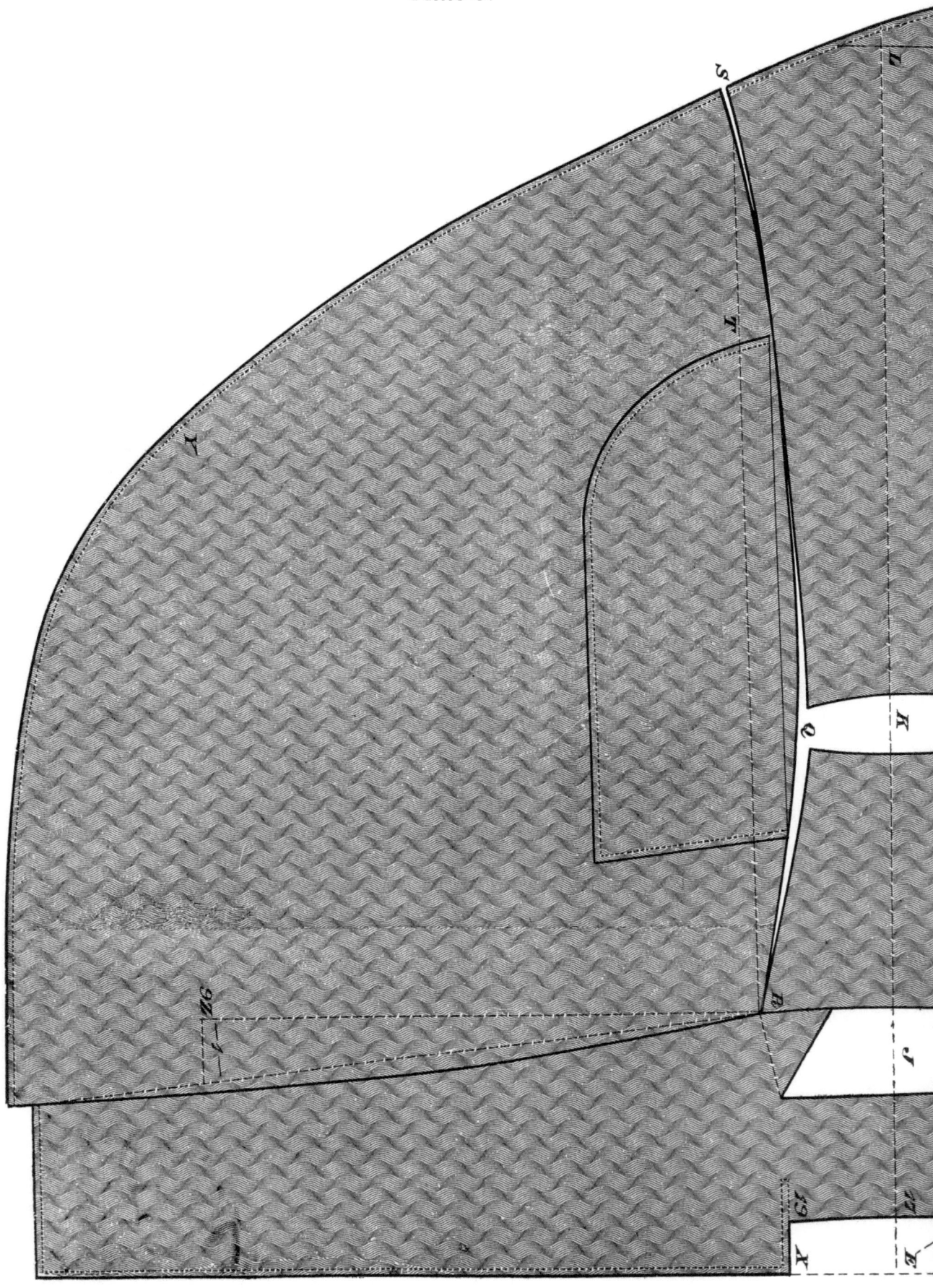

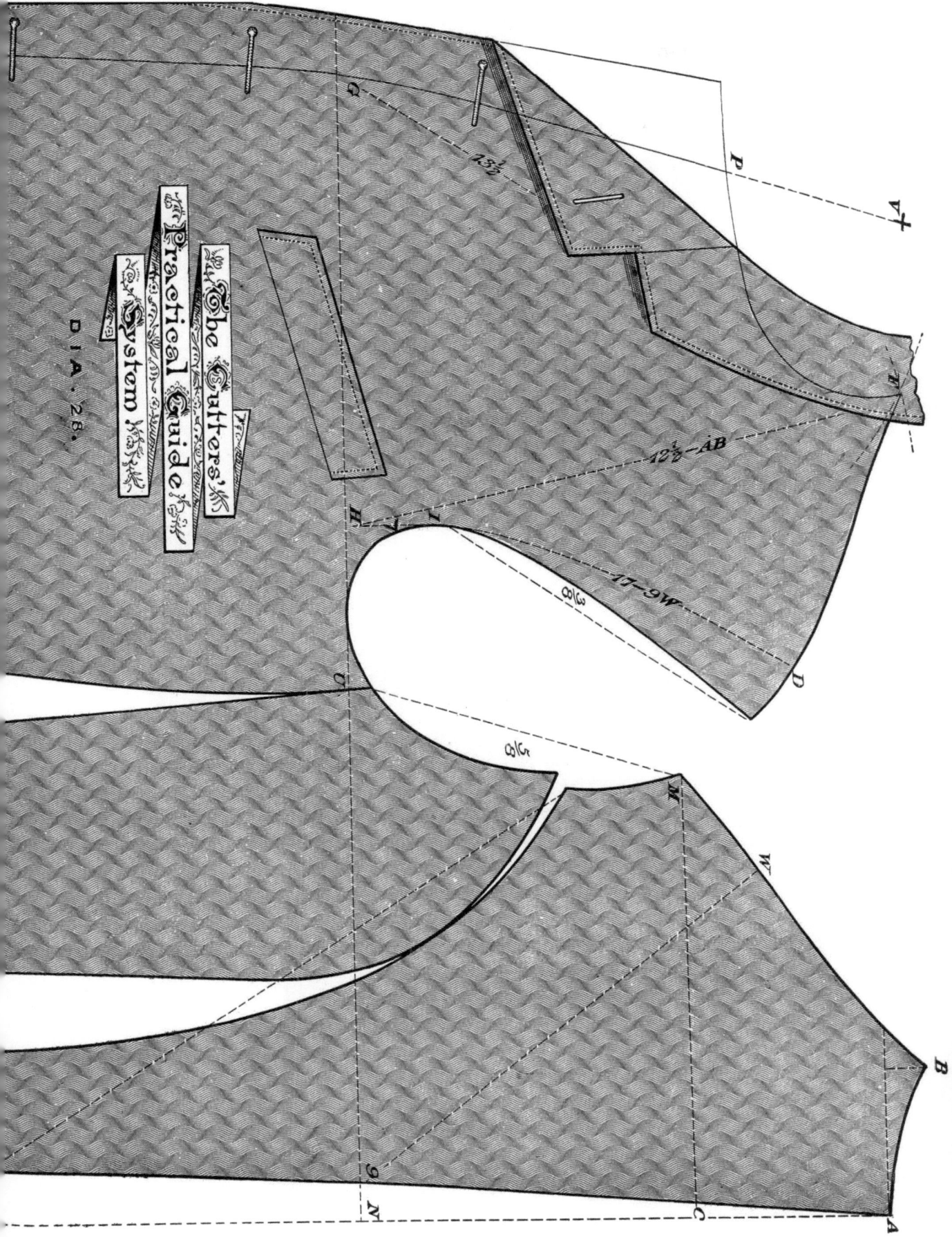

DIA. 28.

The Cutters' Practical Guide System

13½

12½—AB

17—9W

⅜

⅝

71

Plate 4.

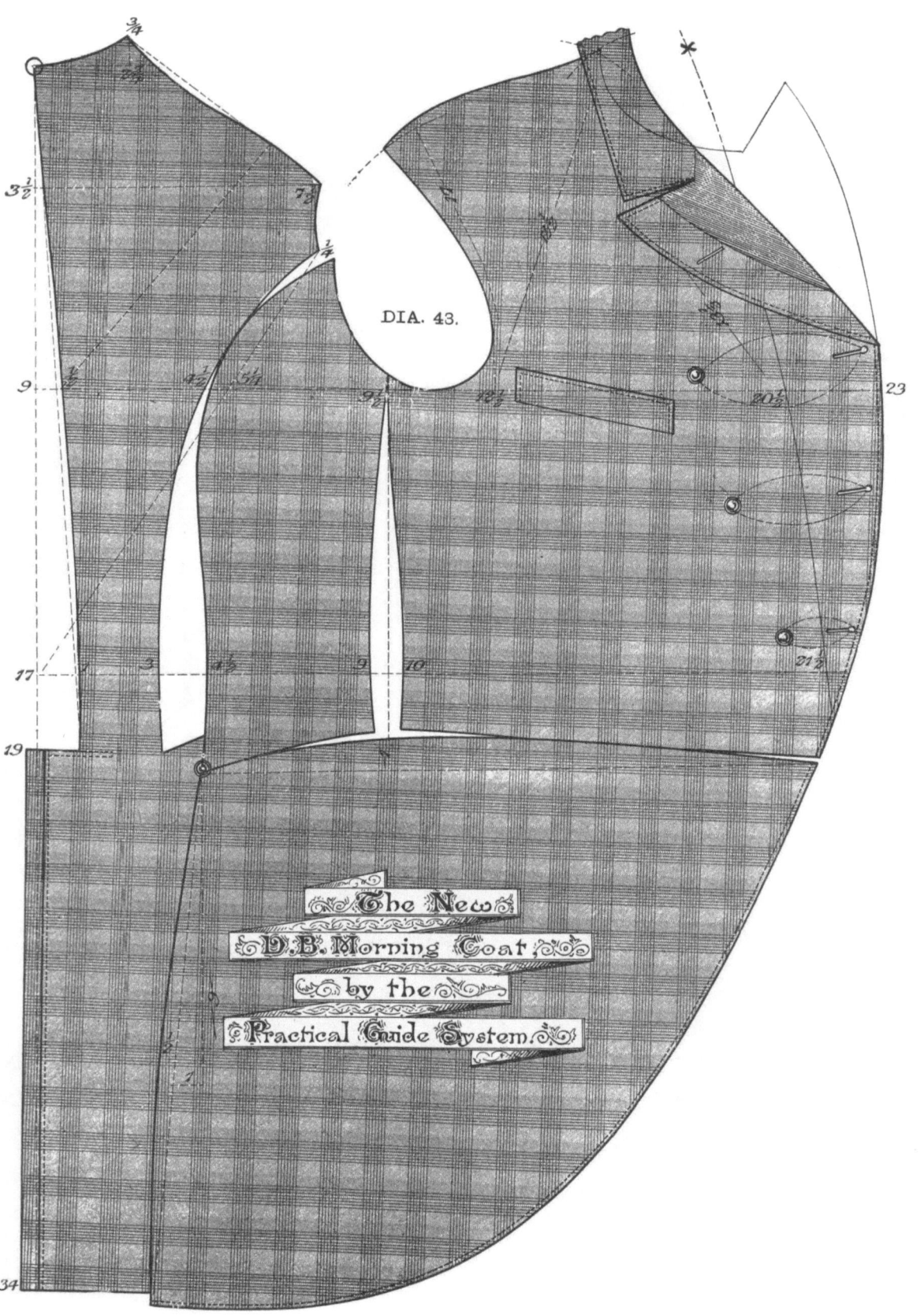

DIA. 43.

The New
D.B. Morning Coat
by the
Practical Guide System

Plate 5.

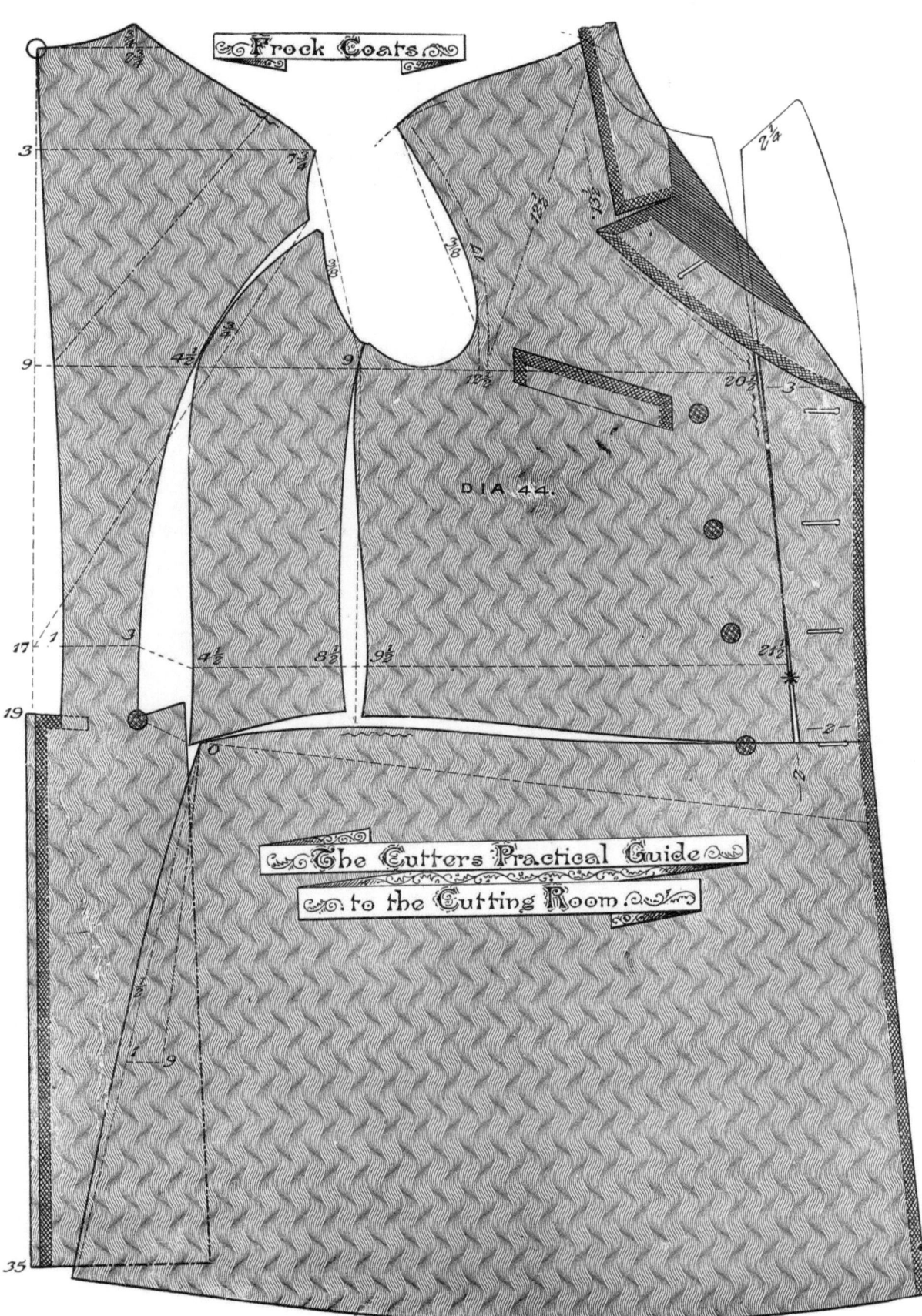

Frock Coats

DIA 44.

The Cutters Practical Guide
to the Cutting Room.

Plate 6.

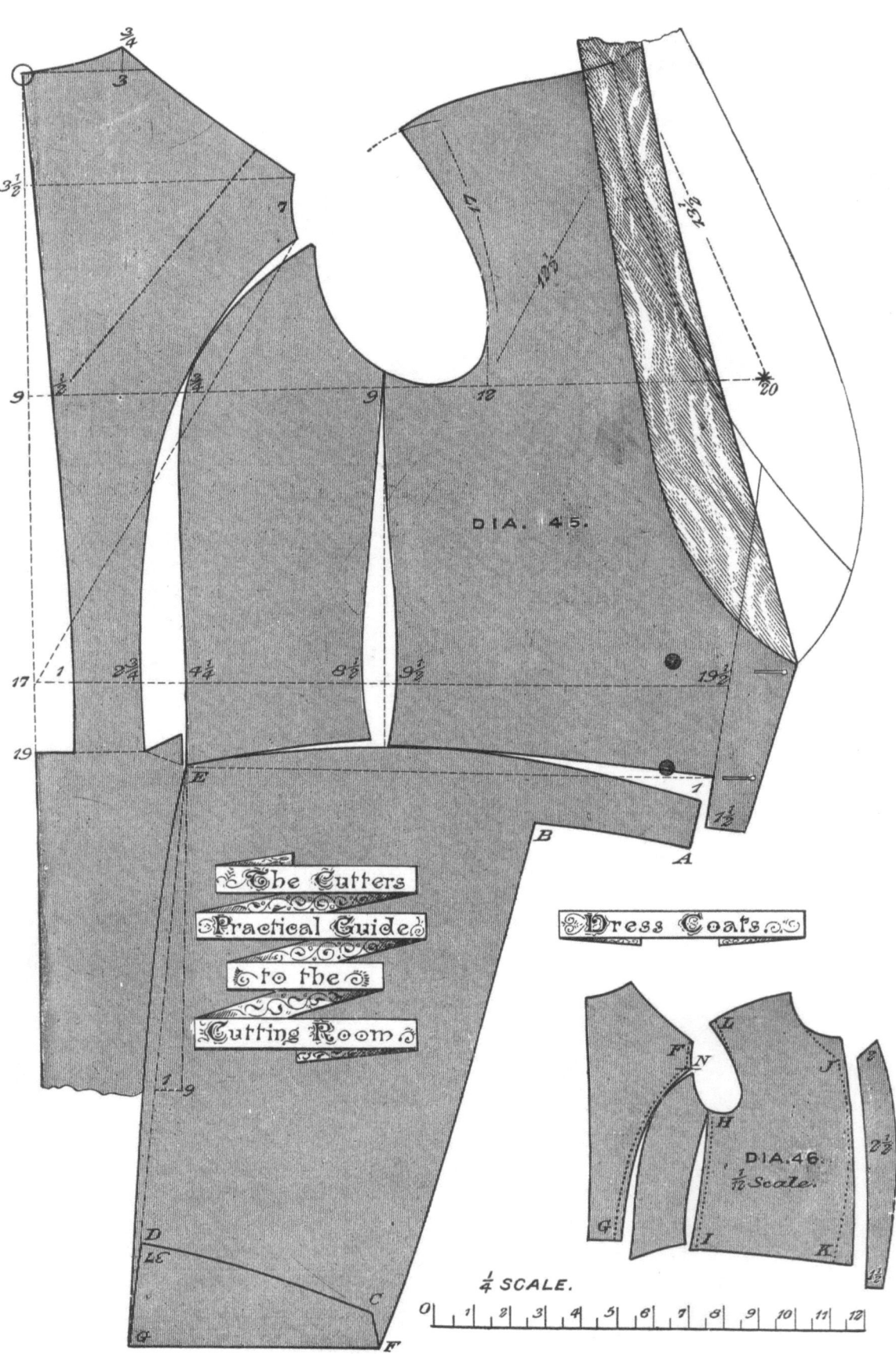

DIA. 45.

The Cutters
Practical Guide
to the
Cutting Room

Dress Coats

DIA. 46.
½ Scale.

¼ SCALE.
0 1 2 3 4 5 6 7 8 9 10 11 12

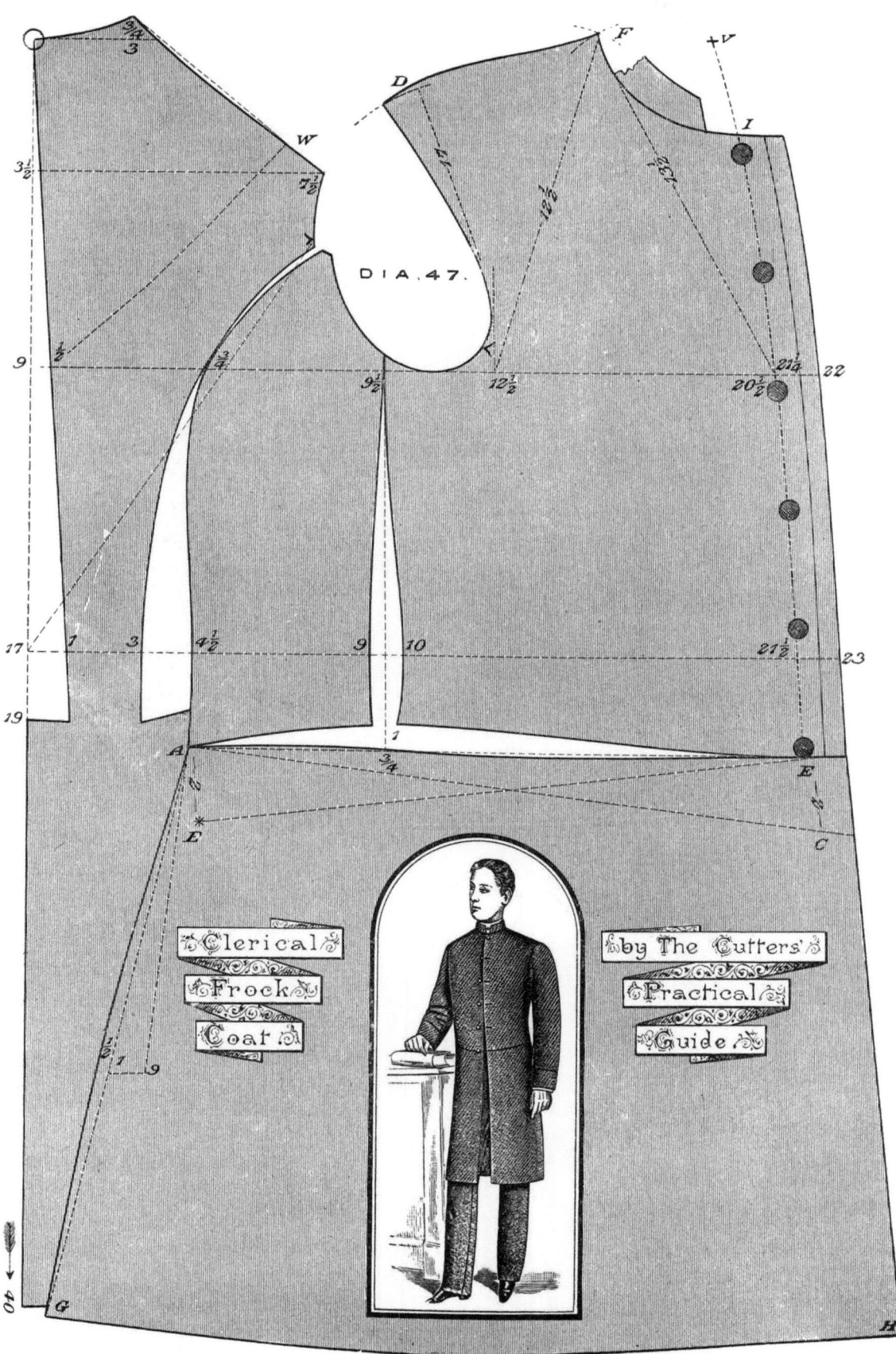

Plate 7.

DIA. 47.

Clerical Frock Coat

by The Cutters' Practical Guide

75

Plate 8.

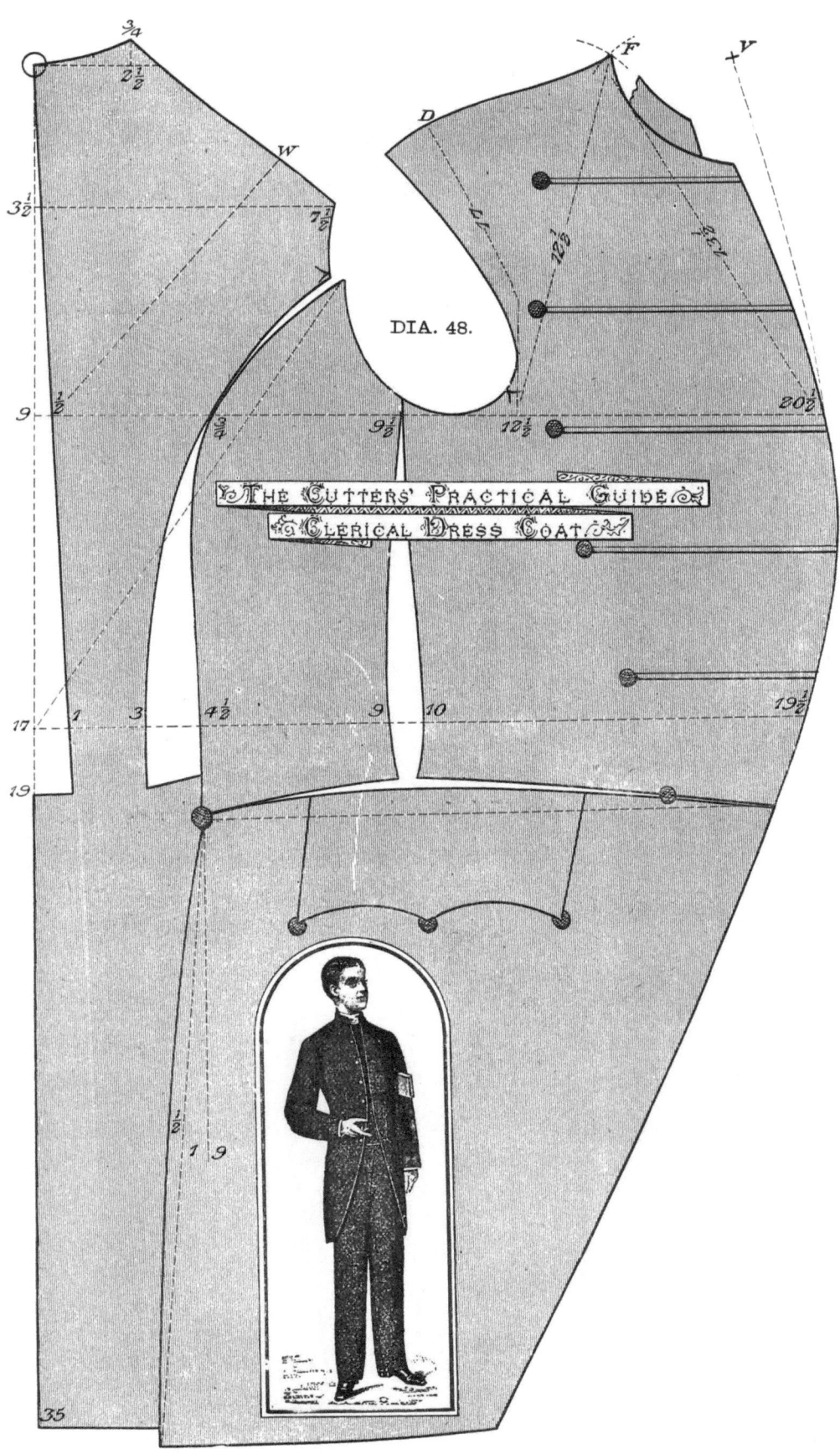

DIA. 48.

The Cutters' Practical Guide
Clerical Dress Coat

Plate 9.

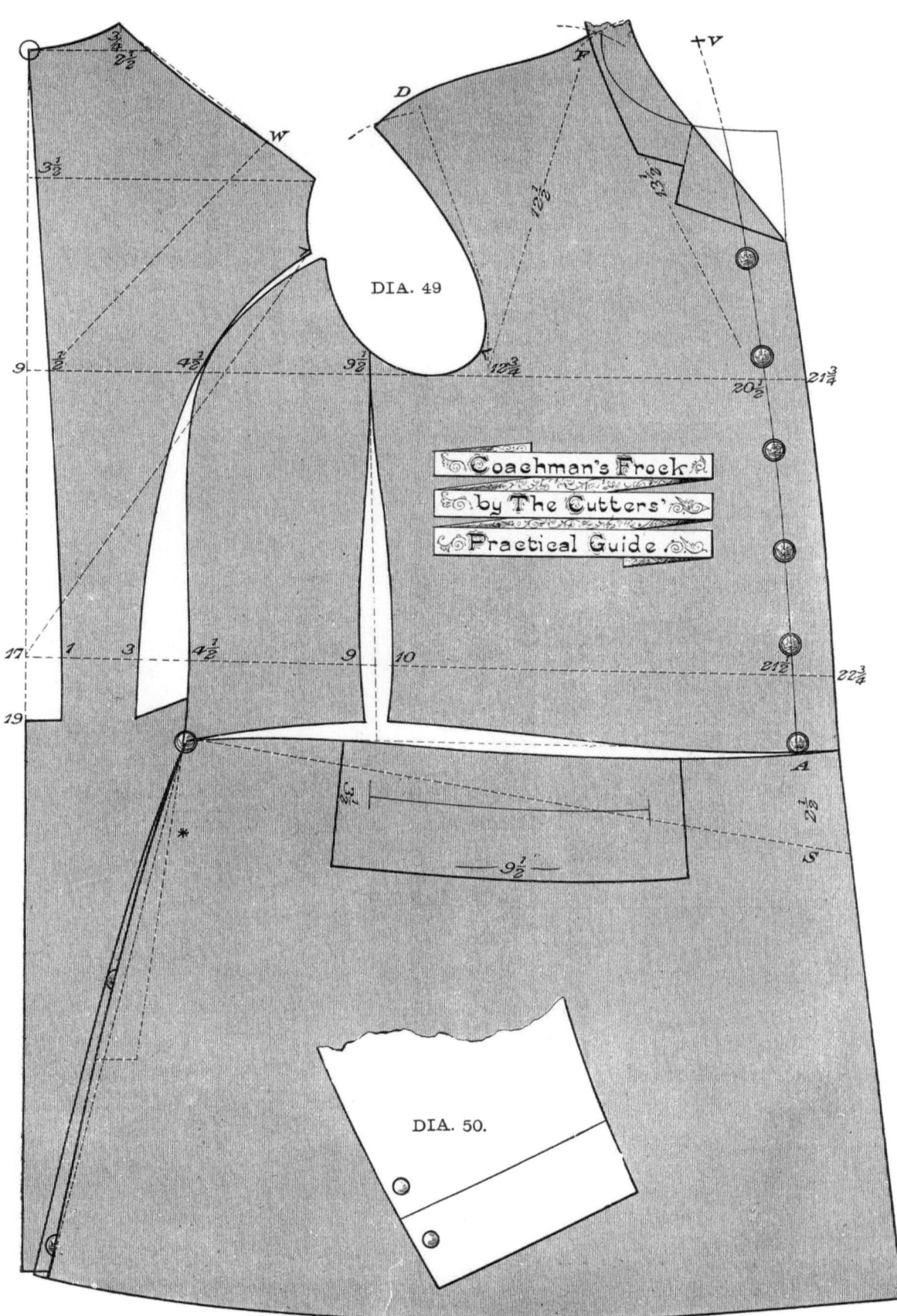

DIA. 49

Coachman's Frock
by The Cutters'
Practical Guide

DIA. 50.

Plate 10.

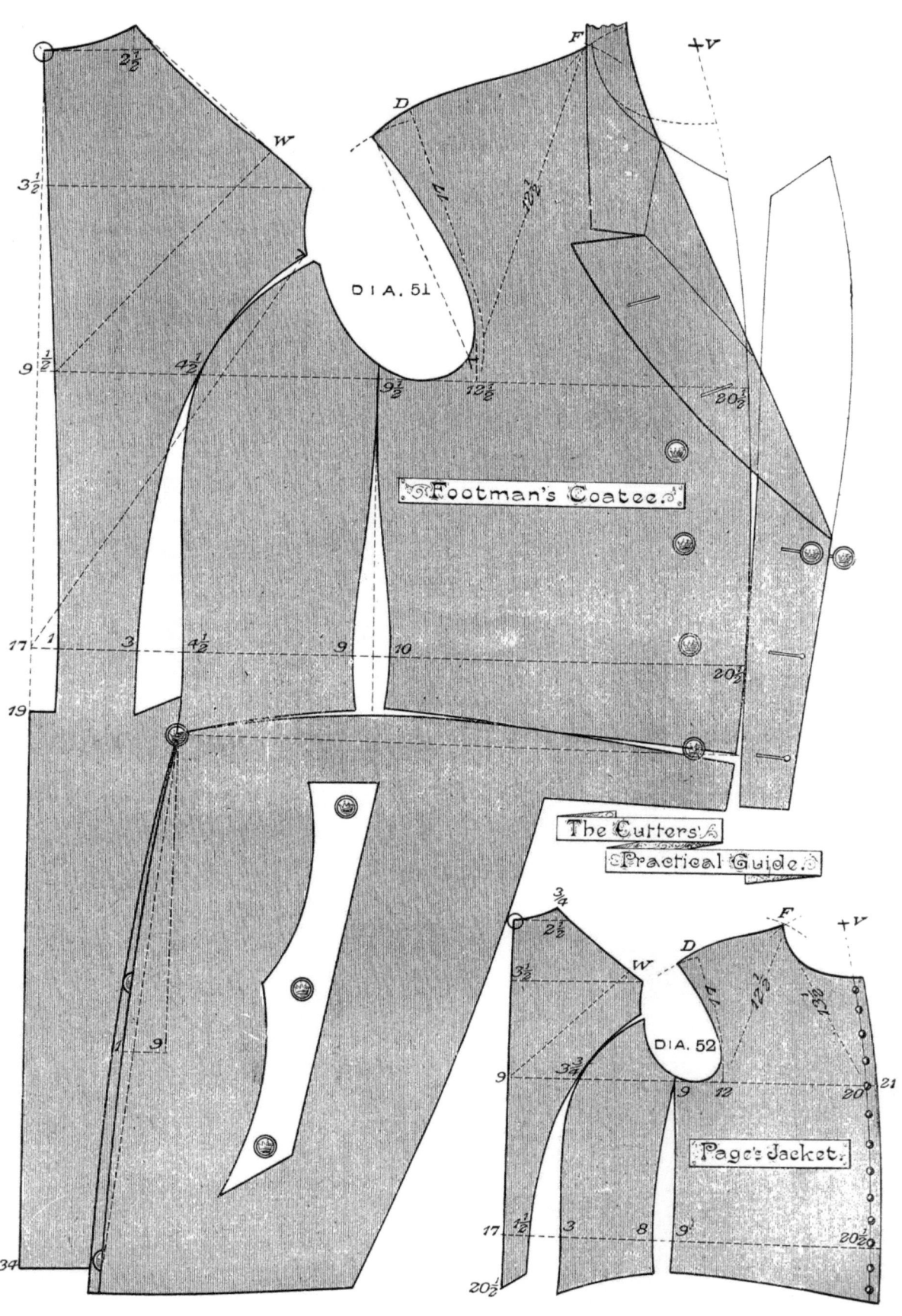

Footman's Coatee.

The Cutters'
Practical Guide.

DIA. 51

DIA. 52

Page's Jacket.

Plate 11.

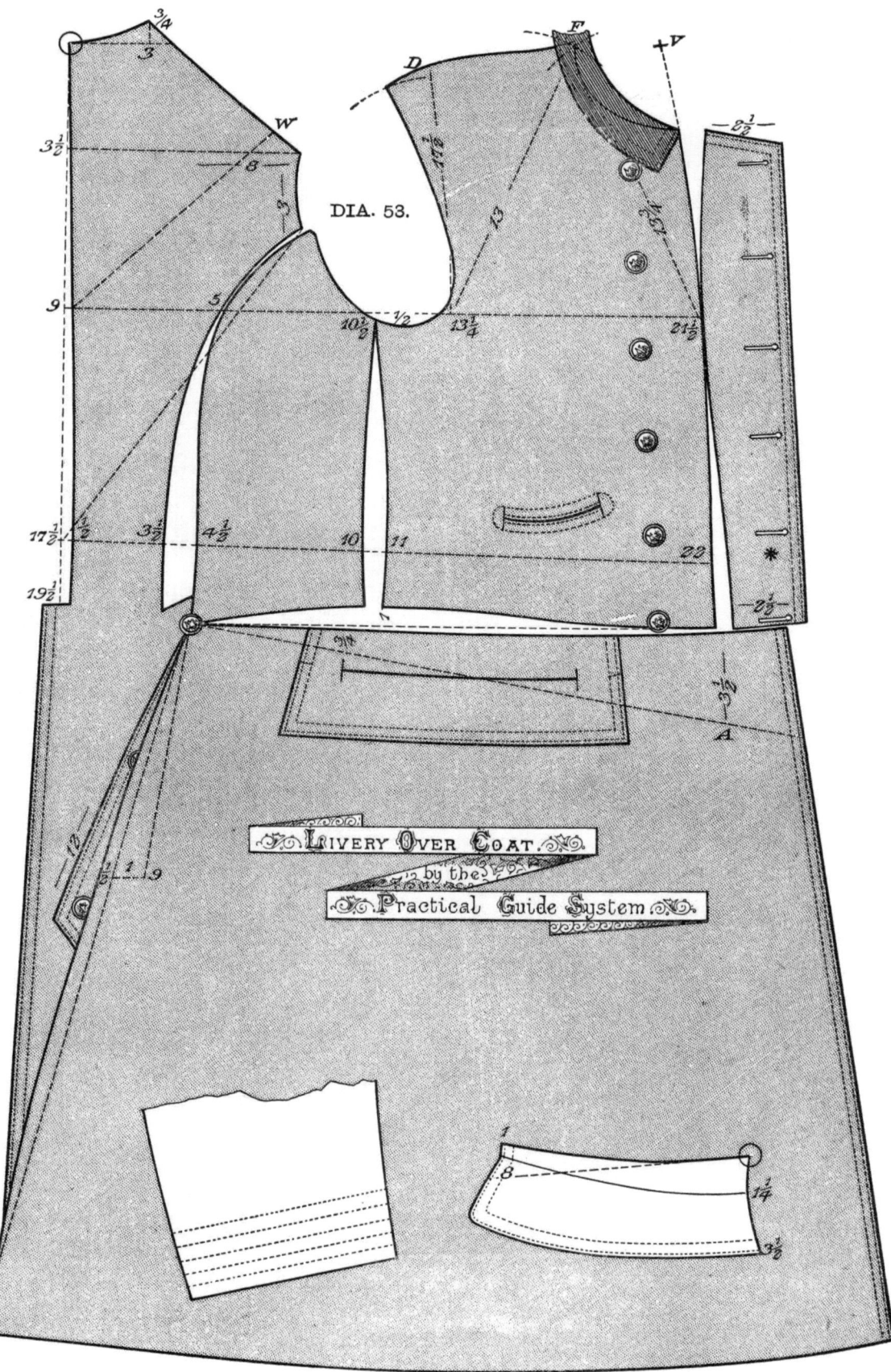

DIA. 53.

Livery Over Coat.
by the
Practical Guide System

Plate 12.

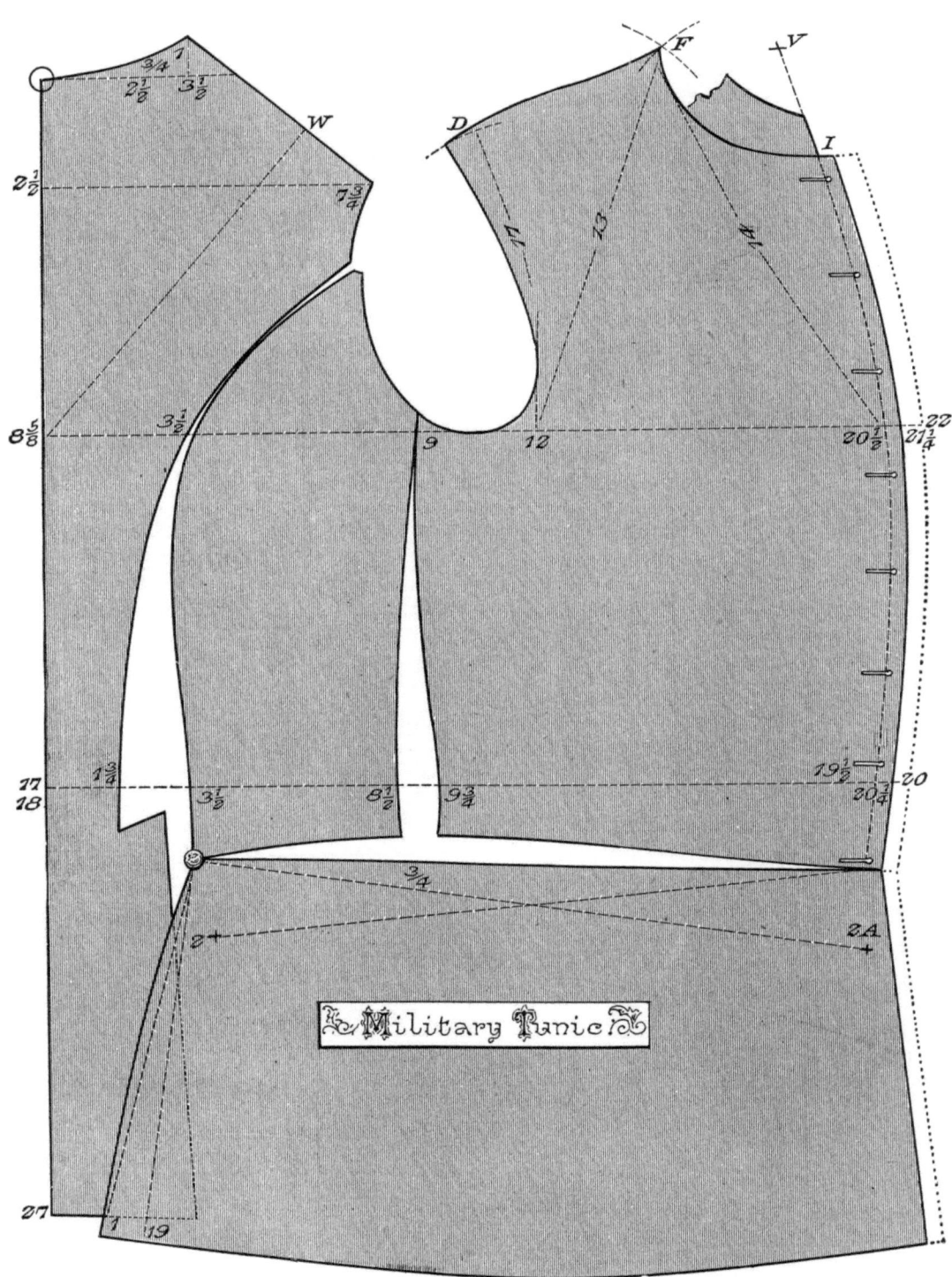

DIA. 54.

Plate 13.

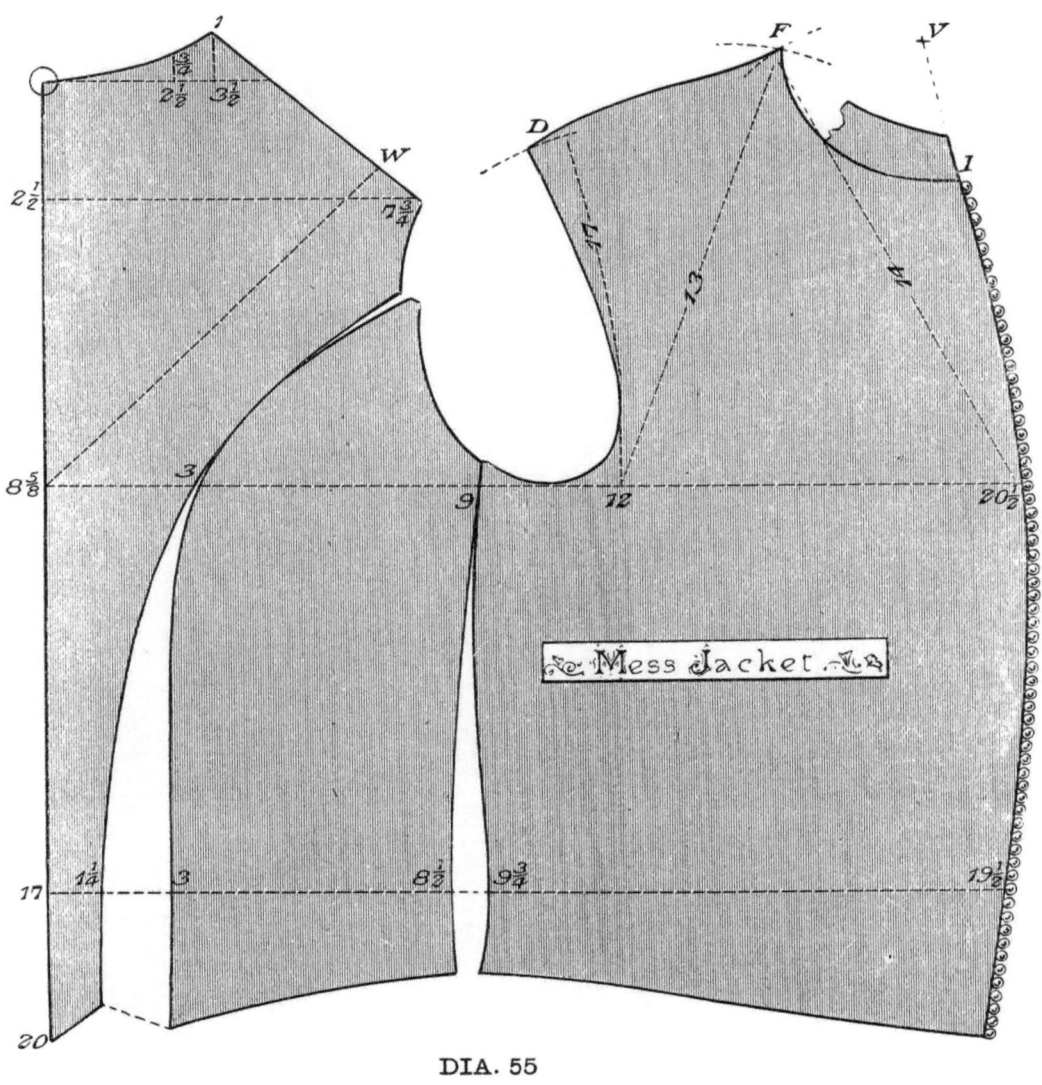

DIA. 55

Plate 14.

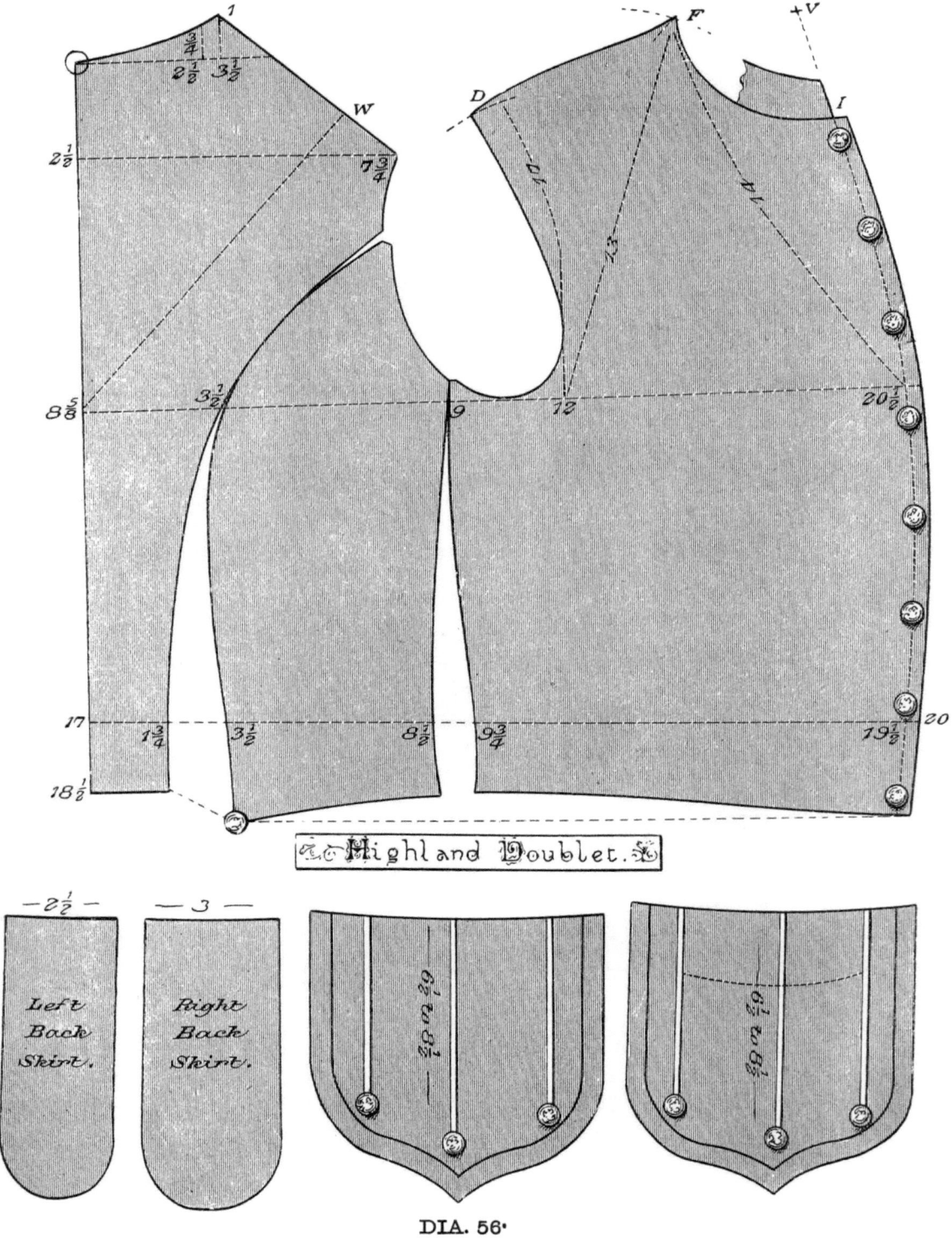

Highland Doublet.

DIA. 56·

Plate 15.

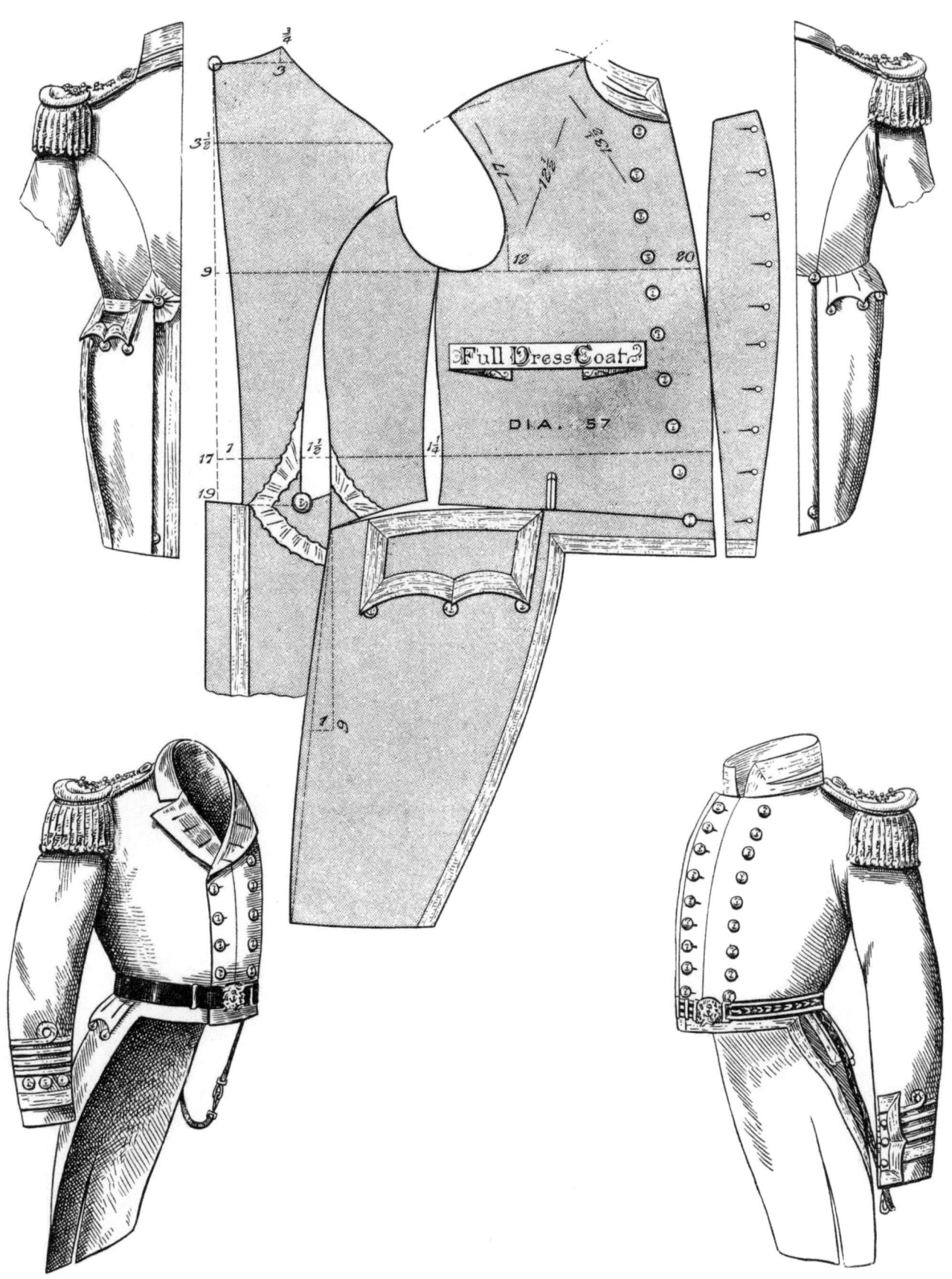

Full Dress Coat

DIA. 57

Plate 16.

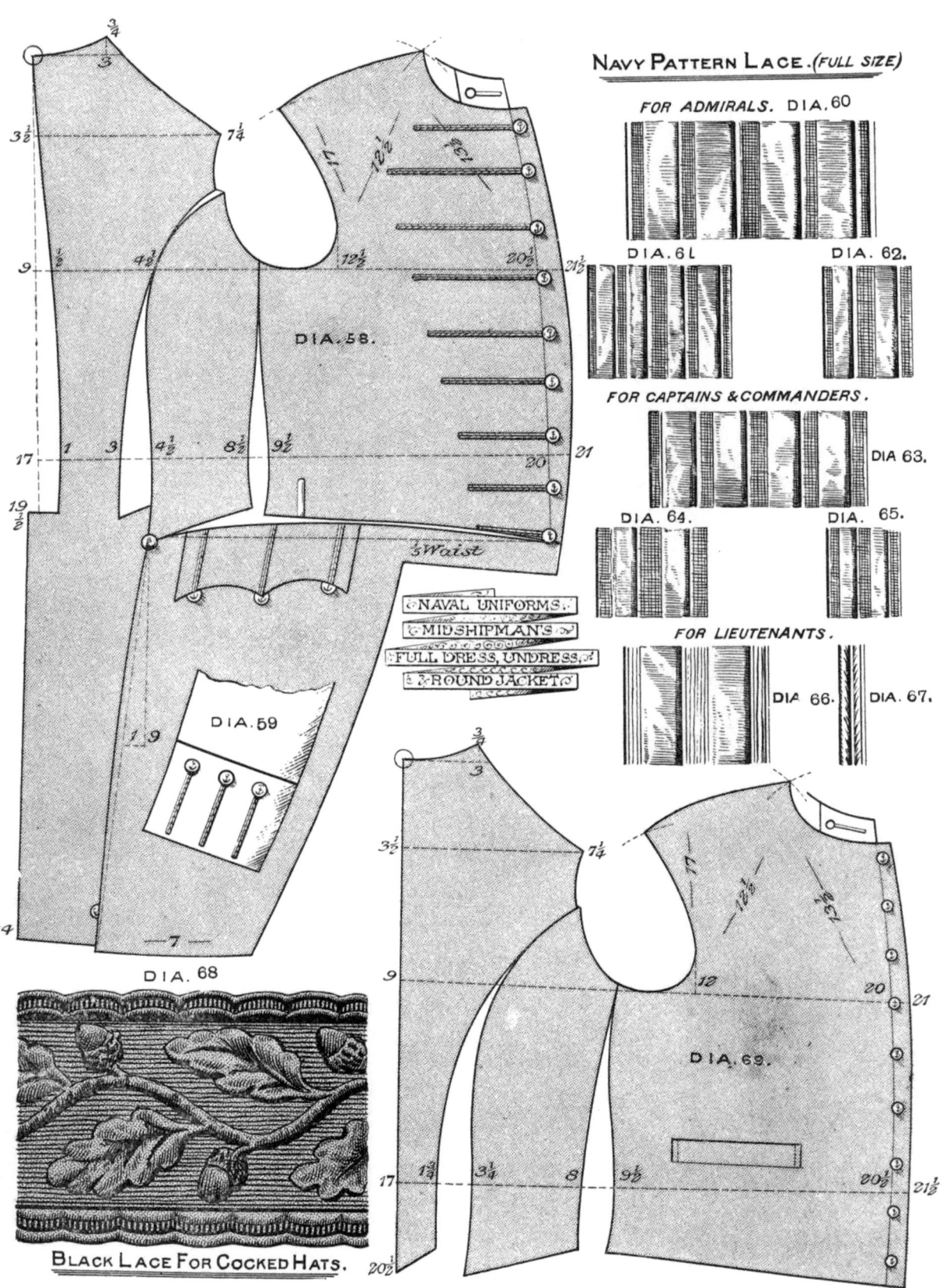

NAVY PATTERN LACE. (FULL SIZE)

FOR ADMIRALS. DIA. 60

DIA. 61   DIA. 62.

FOR CAPTAINS & COMMANDERS.

DIA 63.

DIA. 64.   DIA. 65.

FOR LIEUTENANTS.

DIA. 66.   DIA. 67.

DIA. 58.

NAVAL UNIFORMS.
MIDSHIPMAN'S
FULL DRESS, UNDRESS,
& ROUND JACKET.

DIA. 59

DIA. 68

BLACK LACE FOR COCKED HATS.

DIA. 69.

Plate 17.

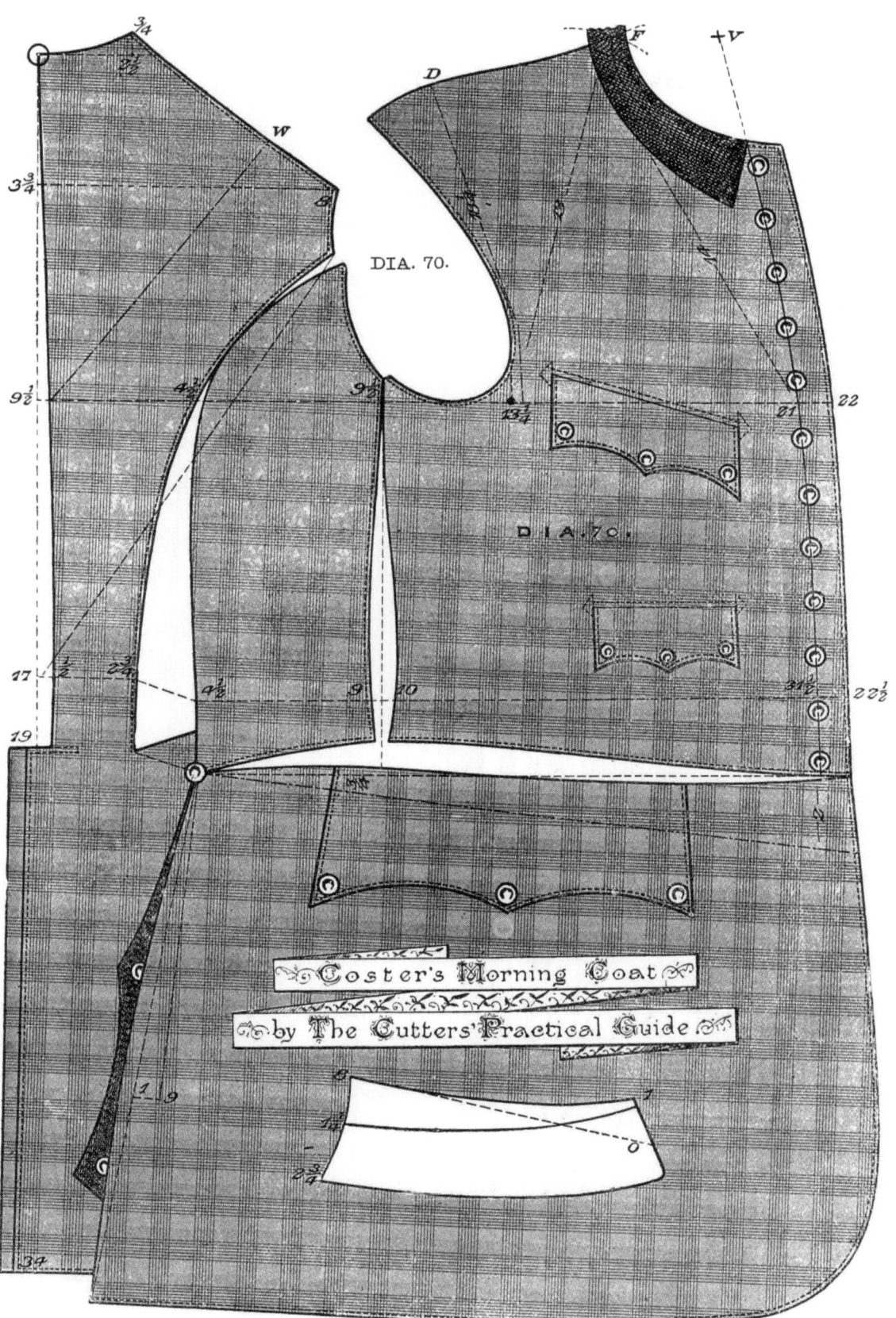

DIA. 70.

Coster's Morning Coat
by The Cutters' Practical Guide

Plate 18.

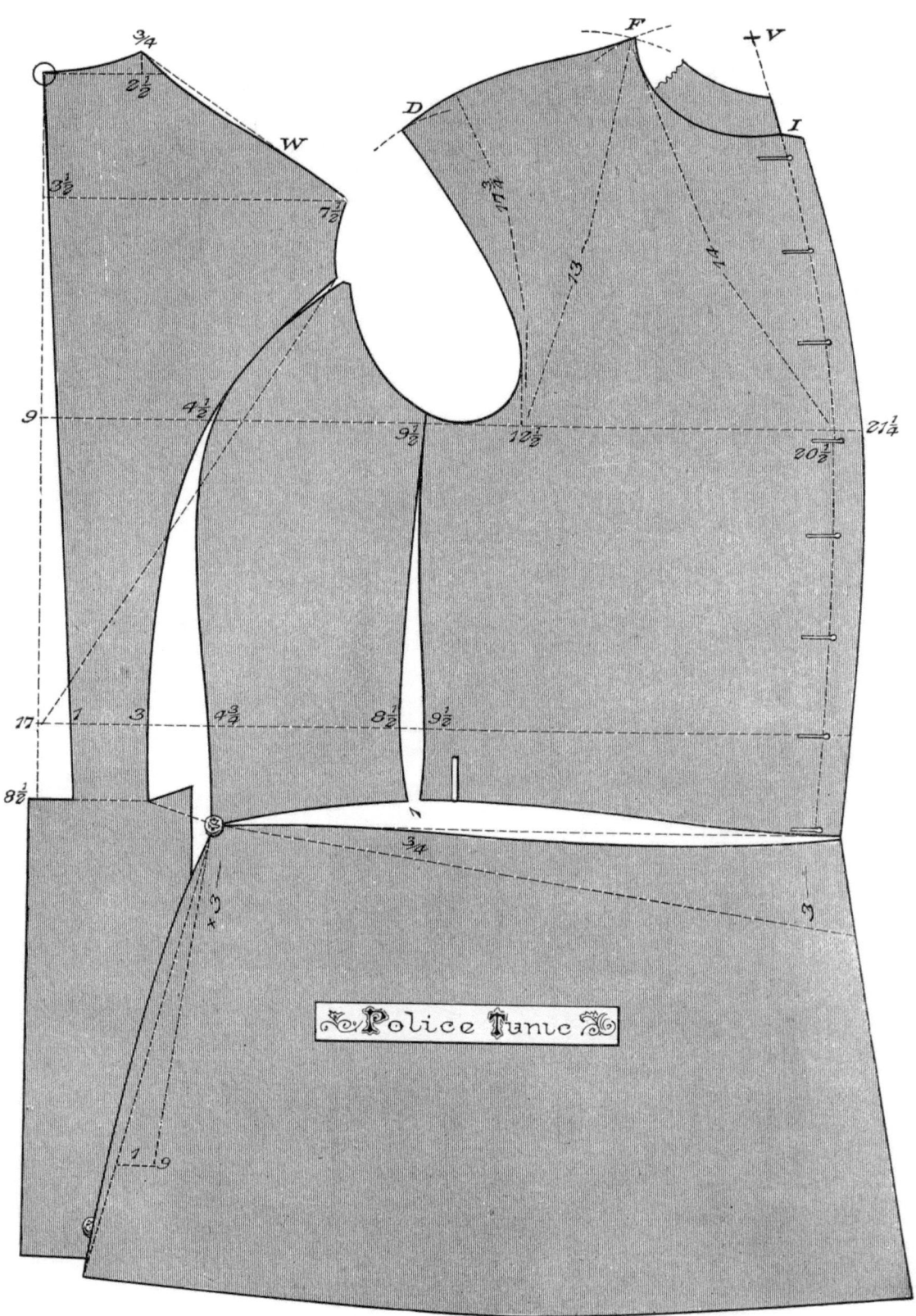

DIA. 71.

Plate 19.

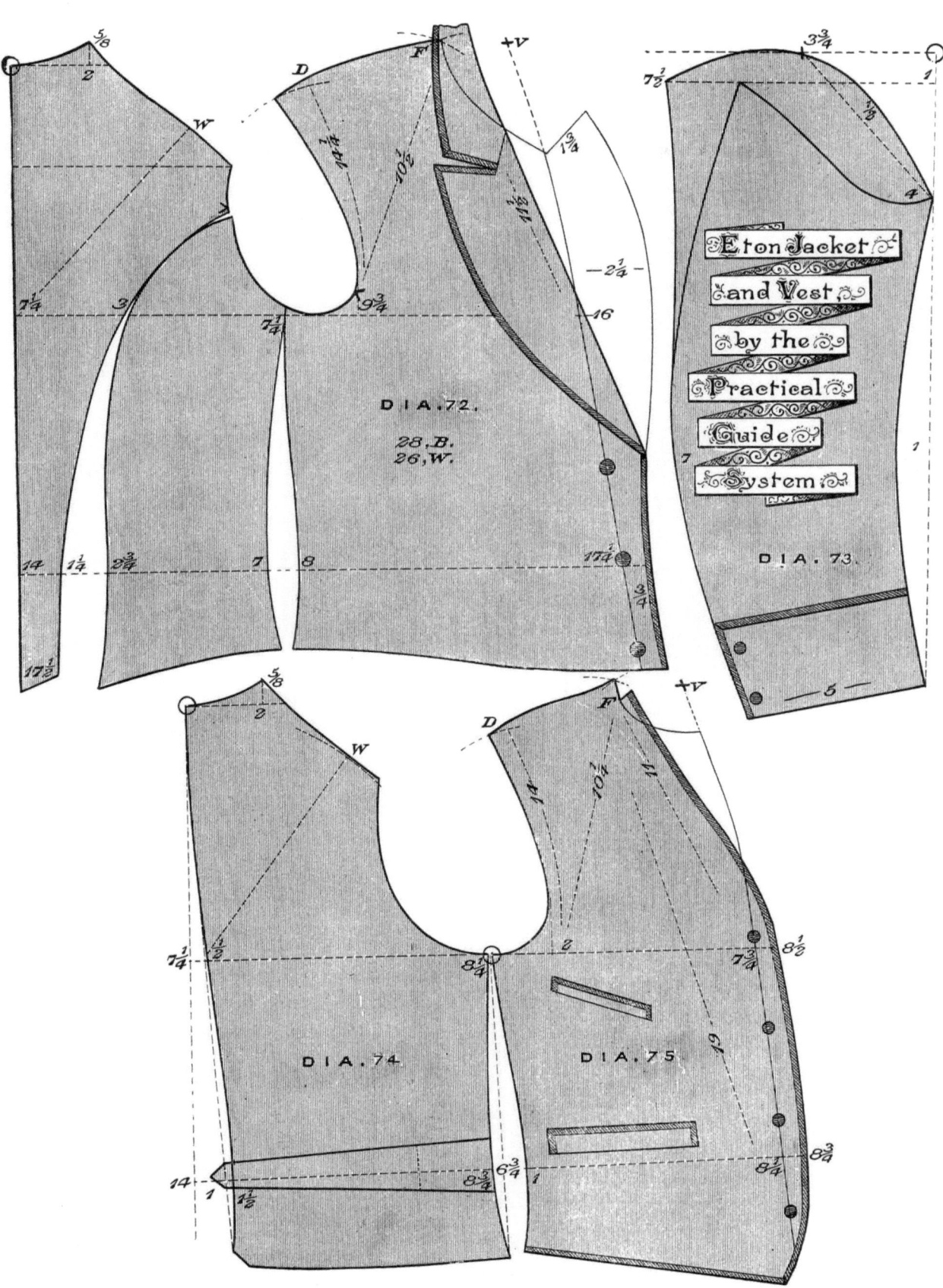

DIA. 72.

28,B.
26,W.

Eton Jacket and Vest by the Practical Guide System

DIA. 73.

DIA. 74

DIA. 75.

Plate 20.

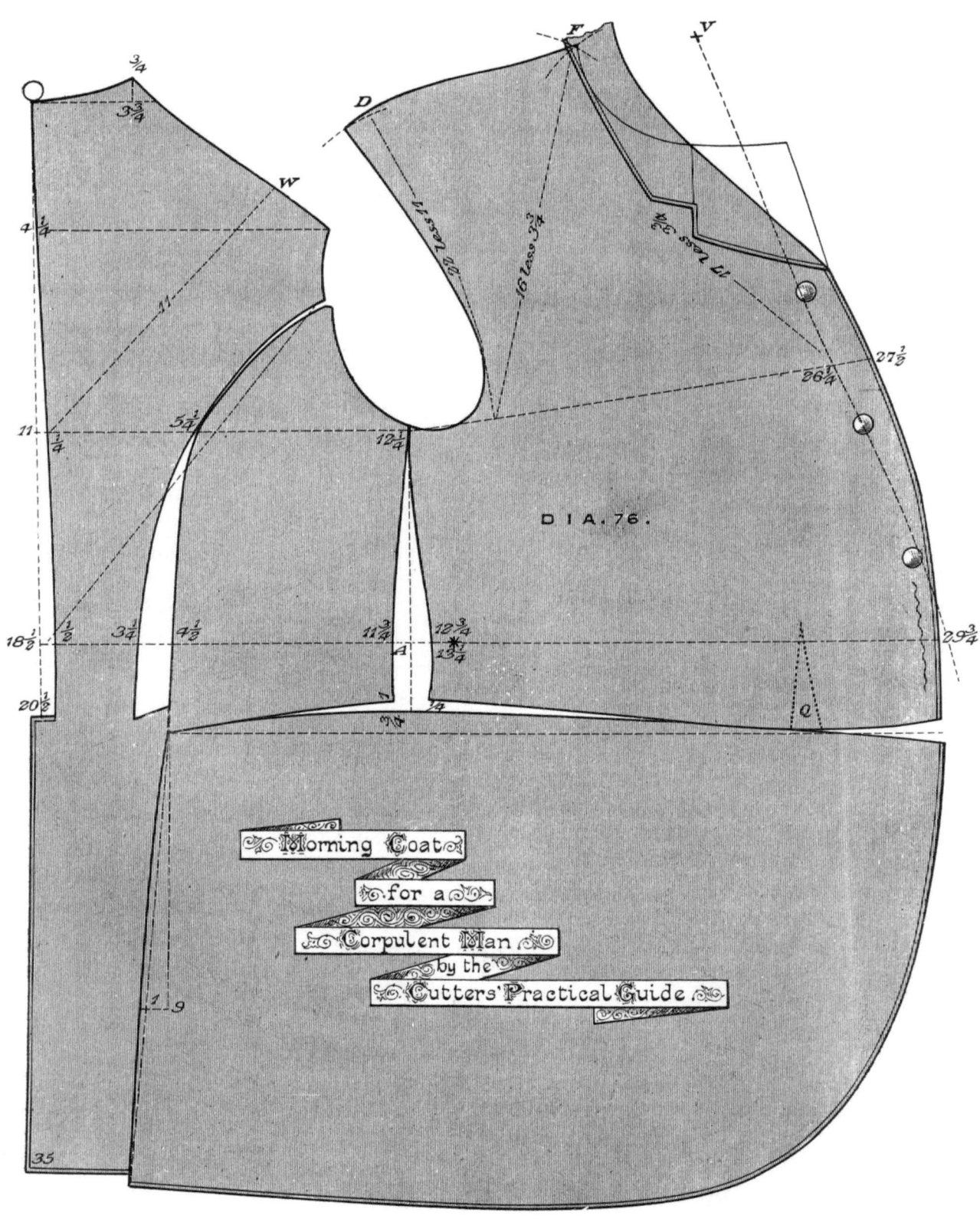

DIA. 76.

Morning Coat
for a
Corpulent Man
by the
Cutters' Practical Guide

Plate 21.

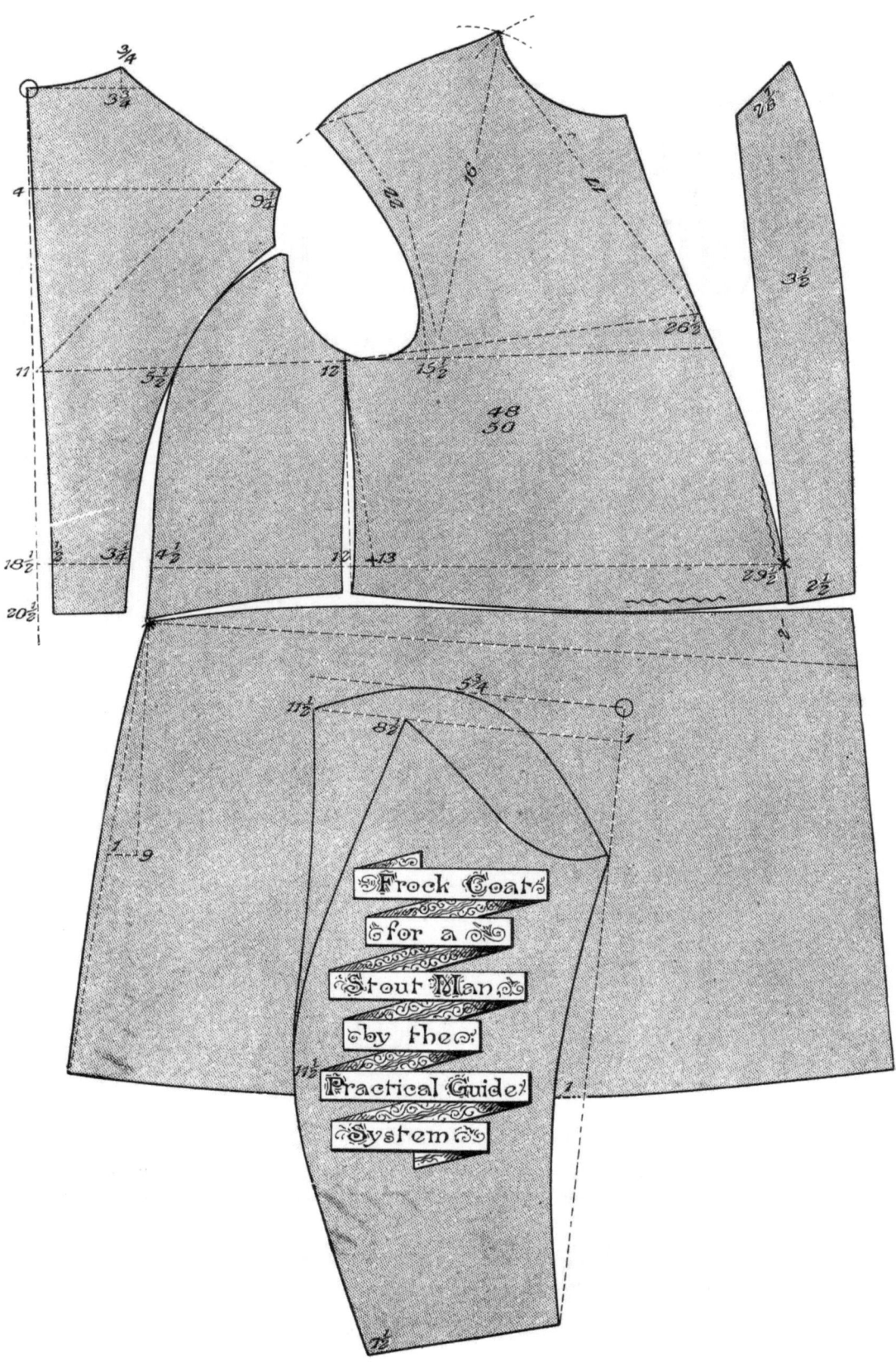

DIA. 77.

Frock Coat for a Stout Man by the Practical Guide System

NOW READY.

Price **2/3**,
Post Free.

Worth **10/6**
At the Least.

THE TAILOR AND CUTTER

SEMI-ANNUAL PLATE OF FASHIONS,

FOR AUTUMN & WINTER, 1898-9.

A SPLENDID PRODUCTION.

THE FINEST BUSINESS-BUILDER FOR THE COMING SEASON THAT ANY TAILOR CAN POSSESS.

ORDER AT ONCE.

Hundreds Disappointed last Season because they couldn't get it.   Thousands delighted by Securing in Time.

The John Williamson Company. Limited. 93 and 94, Drury Lane, London, W.C.